Advance Praise for *A Baptist Among the Jews*

"As another 'Baptist among the Jews' I savored every page of Mary Blye Howe's fascinating and instructive book. Her warm personal approach to a conversation that has often been soured by either bitterness or stiff politeness helps all of us as Christians to take another step toward mending a relationship that is utterly vital to us."
—Harvey Cox, Ph.D., Victor S. Thomas Professor of Divinity, Harvard University, and author of numerous books, including *The Seduction of the Spirit* and *Common Prayers*

"Our increasingly pluralistic world, racked with conflict, hostility, and violence, needs this book. Mary Blye Howe's journey into intimate experiences of searching for truth with Jewish believers proves that enlarged understanding and sharpened insights into people of other faiths can result in enriched appreciation of our own perspectives of God. If we search with our hearts as well as our minds, good things happen. This conservative Baptist came to search for common ground. She emerged with new friendships, broadened perspectives, and a reverent attitude toward God who is larger than the mind of man can comprehend."
—Dr. Jimmy R. Allen, president of the Southern Baptist Convention, 1977–1978

"Mary Blye Howe has written an enlightening book for Christians. It is, however, one that should be read by Jews who, by and large, have lost touch with the power, majesty, and soul-expanding qualities of their faith. Ms. Howe's passion for Judaism, seen through Christian eyes, will be a shot of 'Vitamin J' for any Jew who avails him- or herself of it."
—William A. Gralnick, SE Regional Director, American Jewish Committee

"This is not merely a 'Christian' account of Judaism. It is, more fundamentally, a loving, curious, and insightful account. Mary Blye Howe's debut promises to make a unique contribution to both 'Jewish-Christian relations' and to Jewish-Christian relationships."
—Lauren F. Winner, author of *Girl Meets God: On the Path to a Spiritual Life,* columnist for Beliefnet.com, and contributor to *Christianity Today* and *Books & Culture*

"You will close Howe's book determined to find the kind of enthusiasm for faith she displays on every page of *A Baptist Among the Jews*."
—Colleen Hughes, senior contributing editor, *Guideposts,* and editor-in-chief, *Angels on Earth*

"Some will see this book as the remarkable story of a Christian coming to deeply understand and appreciate Judaism. Others will be impressed by Mary Blye Howe's excellent research and the way in which she, as a good writer, deeply immersed herself in her subject. But essentially it is the story of an author who, through discovering how other people find God, embraces new dimensions of God in her own life.

This book opens the door to a special understanding of one of the world's great religions. It is a wonderful read for those who seek to understand the passion and practice of the Jewish religion."
—Dr. Phil Strickland, director, Texas Baptist Christian Life Commission

"A deeply religious and existential encounter between a faithful Christian and Jews with many outlooks. No conversion from one faith to another here, but a Buberian meeting and encounter where all are transformed, and at the same time remain true to who they are."
—Rabbi Sheldon Zimmerman, Rabbi of Temple Emanu-El, 1985–1996, and president, Hebrew Union College-Jewish Institute of Religion, 1996–2000

"With the disarming passion of a neophyte (but without leaving her own faith behind), Howe plunges into the rich world of traditional Judaism, emerging with jewels that all of us can profit from: a profound sense of God's holiness, an insatiable hunger for and love of God's Word, and an understanding of the importance of ritual and community. Howe's friendship with the Jewish people and her deep spiritual experiences amidst them brings a whole new dimension to her Christian faith, and her winsome story encourages those of us who have yet to embrace our Jewish roots to similarly enrich our journey by crossing the cultural and emotional barriers that so often separate us and seeking to learn from our spiritual kin."
—Kristyn Komarnicki, editor, *PRISM* magazine, Evangelicals for Social Action Committee

"The time has come to move beyond polite tolerance to genuine friendship between Christians and Jews. Mary Blye Howe is an advance scout in this exploration, going deep into the unknown world of Judaism and finding a welcome that bids others to follow."
—George A. Mason, Ph.D., Senior Pastor, Wilshire Baptist Church, Dallas, Texas

"*A Baptist Among the Jews* is an exuberant, uplifting, and inspiring read for all of us who have found ourselves embarking on a spiritual journey. Its pages reveal the author's excellent grounding in Jewish belief and practice, making it one of those rare books that not only engages and absorbs but educates as well."
—Karen J. Prager, Ph.D., A.B.P.P., professor of psychology, the University of Texas at Dallas

A BAPTIST
AMONG THE
JEWS

Mary Blye Howe

FOREWORD BY JOHN WILSON

AFTERWORD BY RABBI LAWRENCE KUSHNER

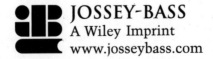

JOSSEY-BASS
A Wiley Imprint
www.josseybass.com

Published by Jossey-Bass
A Wiley Imprint
989 Market Street, San Francisco, CA 94103   www.josseybass.com

Jossey-Bass books and products are available through most bookstores. To contact Jossey-Bass directly call our Customer Care Department within the United States at (800) 956-7739, outside the United States at (317) 572-3986 or fax (317) 572-4002.

Jossey-Bass also publishes its books in a variety of electronic formats. Some content that appears in print may not be available in electronic books.

All scripture quotations, unless otherwise noted, are from *The Tanach,* Artscroll Series/Stone Edition, Mesorah Publications, Ltd., Brooklyn, N.Y., 1996.

Library of Congress Cataloging-in-Publication Data

Howe, Mary Blye.
   A Baptist among the Jews / Mary Blye Howe; foreword by John Wilson; afterword by Rabbi Lawrence Kushner.
      p. cm.   "A Wiley Imprint."
   Includes bibliographical references.
   ISBN 0-7879-6558-8
   1. Judaism—United States—Customs and practices. 2. Howe, Mary Blye—Relations with Jews. 3. Jews—United States—Anecdotes. 4. God (Judaism)—Attributes. I. Title.
BM700.H75 2003
261.2'6'092—dc21   2002156550

Printed in the United States of America
FIRST EDITION
HB Printing 10 9 8 7 6 5 4 3 2 1

CONTENTS

CONTENTS

ACKNOWLEDGMENTS

Thank you to the many Jewish communities, synagogues, and precious individuals in Dallas, Texas, as well as the Kehilath Aish Kodesh in Boulder, Colorado, where I always found a loving welcome. Hesha Abrams, Rabbi Asher Goldschmidt, Karen Prager, Reid Heller, and Joe and Sherry Schusterman, you have played a special role in my life, introducing me to and deepening my love for and understanding of Judaism in its different expressions. I love you all. I'm sure that will be evident throughout the pages of this book.

I'm indebted to friends who read my manuscript in its early stages: Sue Coffman, Karen Prager, Hesha Abrams, Joe Schusterman, Dennie Brown, and Marc Kivel. You caught my errors and offered valuable advice. Reid, thank you for answering dozens of questions! You are a tireless, dear friend.

Wilshire Baptist, what an incredible church you are! There I've found, for the first time, Christians who have not only given me the freedom for spiritual exploration but who have always been supportive, encouraging, and eager to hear about my adventures. My Sunday school class, The Compass Class, will always be especially close to my heart—thank you for your loving involvement in my life.

To my astounding pastor, George Mason, who first opened my eyes to the vast spiritual world that lies outside the narrow one I had always confined myself to and who continues to challenge my heart and mind, you were truly a lighthouse in a dark, foggy sea.

Mom, thank you for passing on your love and talent for writing, for always believing in me, and for rooting for me every step of the way. I'm certain that my dad, who recently left us to dwell more fully in the presence of God, somehow managed to carry copies of all of my articles with him and is now showing them to everyone in the spirit world. To my families, both the one into which I was born and the one into which I married: you enrich my life. Peggy, thank you for being such an intimate part of my spiritual journeys and for your rare and priceless enthusiasm and interest. I love you all.

Michael, what an amazing man and husband you are. It isn't enough to say that you've stuck by me through earth-shattering changes over the past twenty-seven years—you've grown and changed along with me, loved me more deeply each and every year, and encouraged me in every single pursuit I've undertaken, no matter how wild. You've read every word I've written, offered valuable advice, and listened endlessly to my stories and long-winded ideas. Thank you. I love you.

What can I say about you, Mark Kerr, except—Wow! Had I been able to mold, shape, and create the ideal editor, it would have resulted in you. Your excitement over this manuscript, from its initial inception as a mere proposal to its completion, utterly wiped away any insecurities I had about writing this book. Your guidance and advice were invaluable. You are a true gem! Thank you also to other Jossey-Bass editors with whom I've begun to get acquainted: Chandrika Madhavan, Erin Jow, and Joanne Clapp Fullagar—and others whom I hope to get to know in the future. What a great team! What an outstanding publishing house!

FOREWORD

I hated this book. My copy of the manuscript is full of underlining and marginalia in which I carried on a running argument with the author.

I loved this book. Mary Blye Howe's passion for Judaism is joyously contagious; it made me want to dance and praise God.

Not many books inspire such contrary reactions in the same reader. But *A Baptist Among the Jews* is not an ordinary book. It comes at an extraordinary moment in Jewish-Christian relations, the most hopeful in many centuries. And yet while the high-level exchanges between Jewish and Christian scholars and religious leaders are of great significance, they hardly penetrate the world of ordinary believers.

How many evangelical Christians have the faintest idea of what it's like to study scripture as a devout Jew? How many have visited a synagogue to experience Jewish worship? How many evangelicals have even been inside the home of an observant Jewish family?

Enter *A Baptist Among the Jews.* A latter-day Candide, Howe enters the world of Judaism with wide-eyed enthusiasm and a refreshing lack of pretension. It is all fresh and quirky and delightfully new—and so different from what she'd been taught about Judaism in the "strict evangelical church" from which she and her husband fled to a more expansive Christian fellowship. Jews are legalistic? Not at all, Howe protests. When practiced as intended, the Orthodox adherence to dietary regulations and other demanding laws is all about relationship with God: law leads to intimacy. In fact, Howe adds, evangelicals are themselves vulnerable to legalism, with taboos against smoking and drinking and the like.

These are helpful provocations. I hope some bright young independent film director will be alert to the potential of Howe's story, which could become another *My Big Fat Greek Wedding*. But I fear that many evangelicals will not be interested enough to open this book in the first place. They've utterly lost touch with the Jewish roots of their faith; even the Old Testament is increasingly alien territory in many evangelical churches today.

To such Christians, I want to say: Read this book! Feel free to argue with Howe, just as she relishes the fierce arguments over scripture among her Jewish mentors and friends, but don't stop reading. You will experience in these pages a vivid encounter with Jewish women and men who worship the same God you do. You will never think of Judaism in the same way again. And you may very well find your own relationship with God changed and deepened.

But what about the hardest questions that serious Jews and Christians must wrestle with when they consider their common origin in God's revelation of himself to the people of Israel? What about a Jew named Jesus? If (as I believe and affirm daily) he is who the church has always said he is, doesn't the conversation come to a grinding halt?

Not necessarily. At the heart of *A Baptist Among the Jews* is a willingness to enter into fellowship. Thanks both to Mary Blye Howe's chutzpah and to the warmth and generosity of her Jewish hosts, we too are invited.

John Wilson

IN MEMORY OF RIVKA QUISH

A BAPTIST
AMONG THE
JEWS

CHAPTER ONE

Hanging with the Jews

Each Wednesday night, I stand on the front porch of a Hasidic rabbi's home, waiting for him to open the door for me. Usually I'm the first to arrive—his most eager student. "Hello, Mary. Welcome!" he says, inviting me inside and ushering me to the dining-room table where we study.

If Rabbi G. hasn't yet recited his evening prayers, he slips off his jacket and dons a long black coat, placing a black fedora on his head. Then he begins pacing throughout his house, quietly reciting his prayers.

While the rabbi prays, I browse through his massive collection of books, almost all of which are in Hebrew; the rabbi is fluent in Hebrew, Russian, and English. I try, out of courtesy, not to watch him, but it isn't easy. Rabbi G. is about six feet, four inches tall, with huge brown eyes that seem to penetrate right to your soul. The fervor with which he prays, typical of the Hasidic branch of Judaism, fascinates me. Dressed to greet God, the rabbi invites admiring stares.

Soon others begin arriving, and we sit around the table, talking. When Rabbi G. joins us, we begin our study, first delving into the intricate, detailed observance of the Orthodox and *Hasidim* (plural of *Hasid*). Then about 9 P.M., moving into something else, perhaps a mystical interpretation of the current *parsha* (Torah portion) of the week, maybe a study of the writings of the last, deceased, Lubavitcher Rebbe, whom Rabbi G. follows, or possibly something from the Tanya—one of the mystical kabbalistic texts favored by the Lubavitchers.

Most evenings, the group consists of Orthodox and Hasidic males—and me, a female Baptist. Yet they joke and talk with me as if I were one of them. They're respectful and complimentary of my input and questions. My guess concerning their acceptance of me is that they know I'm sincere. I'm not here to try and convert them to Christianity. I'm here to learn. I'm here because I've grown to deeply love Judaism and the Jews. It hasn't always been that way with me, but it is now. The rabbi opens his Hebrew text. I scoot to the edge of my seat.

My love of Judaism began about five years ago. I had returned to school to study philosophy and anthropology and ran across a newspaper article about a Jewish group that studied Jewish philosophy on a monthly basis. I thought it would be a great enhancement to my academic studies. I had never been around observant Jews, didn't know any personally, and so I called the group's leader, Reid Heller, and asked whether it was OK if a non-Jew attended the studies. He responded warmly and enthusiastically.

As it turned out, the group studied more than Jewish philosophy. They studied different classical Jewish texts and, occasionally, a book of the Bible. The group of about fifteen men and women were from all branches of Judaism. Some wore yarmulkes (*kippot,* in Hebrew); some didn't. (At the time, I referred to them as "little hats" because I had no idea what they were called.) Some were highly observant, meticulously following Jewish law; others observed Jewish law less stringently. A woman who acknowledged God's presence in every aspect of life sat next to another woman who was an avowed atheist. It was an eclectic group.

As for me, I felt like I was being transported back in time to the world of the Bible. I had read all my life of ancient Jewish rituals and lifestyles, but now I began to realize how uninformed most Christians are of Jewish ritual and tradition. I had always held vague images in my mind of Jews praying and teaching in synagogues, but it suddenly occurred to me that I had no real idea what went (or goes) on there, either in ancient or in modern times.

Each month, I sat surrounded by men and women bent over Tanakhs (the Hebrew Bible), various commentaries, and other ancient texts. No longer was I experiencing the world of scripture secondhand. I was involved with the people who encompassed that world, whose traditions and rituals pulsate through each of its pages. Rituals that had been practiced for thousands of years were, in some form, still being practiced today by a group of people I had never even bothered to get to know.

My favorite evenings with Reid's group were the ones in which we studied the Bible. Once we spent an entire hour discussing Bathsheba's seductive bath. One of the women in our group suggested that Bathsheba may have actually been engaged in a Jewish ritual, immersing herself in a *mikvah,* when King David spotted her. This launched numerous opinions from the group, each of which Reid led us to carefully consider. When one was exceptionally thought provoking, he'd stop and say, "Let's go with that."

We tackled the passage, as we always did, from every conceivable angle but never in a merely intellectual manner. We'd look

3

at its history, its philosophical significance, and its cultural relevance—for starters. Numerous interpretations might be offered,
and all were respected, chewed on, dissected, and tossed about.
Dozens of ancient and modern rabbis' writings would be recalled.
Someone would bring up a mystical approach; others would point
out the play on a Hebrew word or the modern implications of the
text.

Rabbi Lawrence Kushner perhaps says it best: In the Jewish
community, he explained, "the Torah or Scripture is expounded,
interpreted, plumbed, allegorized, manipulated, massaged, psy-
choanalyzed, inverted, sliced, and diced. There is no one correct
interpretation. Judaism may begin with a book, but it ends in the
clouds."[1]

Because Reid let us know ahead of time what we'd be studying the following week, several group members came prepared
with piles of texts that shone light on any troublesome spots. I loved
watching them lean over a text, fingers humming along the
Hebrew lines as they read one of the three or four languages some
of them were fluent in.

In Jewish hands, scripture vibrated and pulsed into life. I felt
the passion of the Hebrew God in a fresh way, heard the cry of the
prophets' voices with a new force. The world of the Greek
Testament[2]—Jesus himself—began to wiggle out of the Christian-
ized world the Western church has created and emerged in Judaic
splendor.

Although I knew that these Jews were modern and that they
acquired their information the same way I did—by reading about
the ancient world—they, unlike me, still *lived* aspects of the religious life described in scripture. They still practiced rituals that my
own religion had discarded in its belief that such "graceless" activities were no longer necessary.

This group—then my only representation of Judaism—was connected to the Bible, which was written to and by and for the Jews, in a way I would never be. Regardless of how much we've Westernized scripture, I was smacked with the reality that my Bible was Jewish from start to finish.

Today, with a number of years and hundreds of experiences later, I'm amazed at the way the Jews have transformed me. At the time I began studying with Reid's group, I was in my mid-thirties and had only been out of a strict evangelical church for two years. My husband, Mike, and I had been devoted Christians since we'd married a few months out of my teens; we were attracted to the more conservative edge of evangelical Christianity because of our past drug and alcohol abuse.

During those years, I was so legalistic that I had once canceled my subscription to a magazine because it condoned women working outside the home. Another time, taking communion at a friend's church, Mike and I panicked when we realized they used real wine. In the backseat of our 1968 Camaro, I carried a small box of evangelistic tracts, handing them out to every person with whom I came into contact.

Growing up, I had a vague notion from my church and the Greek Testament (the only source of information I had about Jews or Judaism) that Jews loved rules and had little heart or passion for God. Although I would much later hear that some Christians believed the Jews were "Christ killers," I never heard this personally; the churches I attended believed that Jesus gave his life freely.

Although I hadn't personally encountered any hostility toward the Jews, there was an almost complete lack of knowledge within the churches I attended. In our eyes, Jews followed rules while Christians were passionate about God. God had done everything he could to get them to wake up, to love him, to acquire an understanding of what he wanted, but their hearts were too hard to hear the good news.

What an awakening I was in for. As I began studying and worshiping with the Jews, they would begin to influence every aspect of my spiritual life. The box I had kept God in for so many years would burst open. My experience of prayer would be profoundly deepened. My life would be imbued with a passion for and understanding of ritual and the Bible raised to new heights of symbolism and meaning.

The Jews have taught me that life on earth, not just heaven, matters immensely. They've restored my belief in miracles and helped me to see that God is in everything and everyone. Worshiping with the Jews has plunged me into an intimacy with God that continues to astound me, deepening my love and passion for this Being in a way I never imagined.

Although I studied regularly with Reid's group in the library of the Jewish Community Center, I had not yet ventured into a synagogue. This first adventure in Jewish worship and prayer, in contrast to study, came when my church was invited to participate in an interfaith service at one of the largest Reform temples in the United States.

On that Friday evening, the synagogue was packed. Our Baptist choir sang a hymn from the synagogue's balcony, followed by a psalm in Hebrew from the Temple Emanu-El choir. My pastor, George Mason, gave the benediction for the service.

The following morning, George led the study that preceded Temple Emanu-El's prayer service. Jews and Christians mingled at the tables, and I was thrilled when I noticed two friends from Reid's study group. Soon the rabbi moved to the microphone, trying unsuccessfully to get the crowd to quiet down. "They don't listen to me," Rabbi Zimmerman sighed, "but when Mason gets up here, they'll hush."

Before George got up to speak, Rabbi Zimmerman spent a few minutes "consoling" his congregation about our presence. Because some Christians have spent so many years trying to convert Jews—violently, subtly, deceptively, boldly, by whatever means available—it's difficult for many Jews to feel comfortable with us.

Rabbi Zimmerman assured his congregation that he understood how hard it would be for them to even hear Jesus' name mentioned in the synagogue, as Jesus had been pushed on them in so many ways for so many centuries. Yet in order for healing to take place, the rabbi continued, we must listen to one another, respecting each other's faiths and beliefs, realizing that not all Christians, not even all Baptists, target Jews for conversion. When you hear George talk about Jesus, Rabbi Zimmerman said, please understand he isn't proselytizing; he is explaining the Christian faith.

George's text was the Exodus chapter that preceded the giving of the Ten Commandments—a passage on the calling of the Jews. As George plunged into the text, everyone grew quiet, listening attentively. Occasionally, Rabbi Zimmerman would leap from his chair and comment on something George said. The two men would joke and banter, gripping hands, then engage in side-locked embraces as they discussed their views. Their friendship was obviously close and sincere.

For me, the service evoked an even deeper fascination with Judaism. Although the Saturday morning study was enlightening, my mind was still on the evening before. I had never been inside a synagogue, never seen the beautiful ceremony of the opening of the ark where the large, ornate Torah scrolls are kept, never heard the rhythmic chanting of Hebrew by hundreds of Jews deeply in love with God. Again, everything reverberated with a biblical intimacy that I knew belonged uniquely to the Jews.

Not long after this weekend, I woke up wondering how the Orthodox worshiped. Although a Jewish friend had advised me to take someone along who knew the order of the service, I preferred to attend alone. I wanted to feel my own way along, to absorb the atmosphere of the service without distraction. And I wanted to reflect on it on the way home by myself. I explained this to my cautious friend. "Go for it," he said to me.

I chose a "Traditional synagogue," which differed slightly from an Orthodox one in that, while it provided separate seating for men and women, there's no separation with a *mechitza,* or curtain. In addition, space is provided for men and women to sit together if that's what they prefer. In a true Orthodox setting, sitting together isn't an option.

I slipped in early and sat in the back, as I had absolutely no idea what to expect. In the foyer, the men removed their black fedoras and donned *kippot* (plural of *kippah*), the small head covering traditionally worn by Jewish men; in more liberal synagogues, women sometimes wear them.

The service began with everyone opening prayer books. A congregant stood next to a large flip chart in the front of the sanctuary, so when the rabbi skipped from one section to another in the prayer book, worshipers would know what page they were supposed to be on. I silently read the English translation provided alongside the Hebrew.

As people wandered in, one by one, and took their seats, the men began to chant and pray, rocking back and forth in fast, jerky motions—a movement that is supposed to increase concentration. During the prayer service, the rabbi, assisted by two other men, carefully removed the deep-blue, velvet-covered Torah scroll from the ark.

As the rabbi moved down the aisles with the Torah, the men and women crowded to the edges of the pews. Several rushed to the front of the synagogue, so eager were they to touch and kiss the Torah. The men reverently grazed the Torah with their prayer tassels, then brought the tassels to their lips. Some of the women lightly brushed the Torah with their fingertips or prayer books, then raised them to their lips. Others bent to kiss the Torah itself. I remembered a woman from Reid's group who had once said, "We love the Torah! We kiss the Torah!" Now I understood what she meant.

Despite the different ideologies of Jews regarding the Torah, it is love of these books of Moses—the first five books of our shared Testament—that most closely unites the Jewish people. Everywhere in the world, in every synagogue, each Saturday morning, the same Torah portion is read.

As I followed along, I was bathed in worship and prayer, even though the service, as is typical of Orthodox and Traditional services, lasted three hours and was almost entirely in Hebrew.

Each section of prayer represents a closer and closer approach to God, which the Hasidim describe as "moving into a different world." When the *Shema*—the most important prayer in Judaism—is recited, worshipers, at least in Orthodox circles, cover their eyes with their hands. This symbolizes that they are entering

God's presence. The *Amidah* climaxes the prayer service, reflecting the mystical belief that worshipers have entered the highest world. They are in the presence of God. It's the only prayer that is whispered—a sign of awe and respect at moving so close to an utterly holy Being.

As I've understood more about the Jewish prayer service, it has taken on added meaning. However, I've found that it isn't necessary to understand a word of Hebrew or to comprehend a single aspect of the service to experience the presence of God. Each time I've attended, I've felt a charged atmosphere, an overwhelming sense of holiness and of love and connection with God. The Jews have come to pray, to encounter God, to worship; spiritual energy permeates the synagogue.

Although I was captivated by everything and everyone around me when I attended my first Traditional Jewish service, I was particularly absorbed in watching an elderly man sitting in the pew across from me. Although members came in late and left early and, at some informal parts of the service moved across the aisles to chat with one another, this man never once looked up from his prayer book. I don't think he was even aware that anyone else was in the synagogue, other than God.

Even during prayers, when a smattering of the congregation failed to join in, the old man didn't miss a word. He was utterly absorbed in God, his voice rising and falling, melodic and intense. The look on his face was one I've seen on faces of ecstatic mystics. I couldn't take my eyes off him. Although I was afraid he might sense me staring, he never did, for he sensed nothing but the presence of God.

Months later, when I was more comfortable in my friendship with the Jews I'd come to know, I began asking around to find out who this man was. One friend thought he knew and gave me a phone number. I called, but it wasn't he. I returned twice to the synagogue but he wasn't there. I began to think he might have been an angel. In fact, I'm sure he *was* an angel, even if he was also a flesh-and-blood human being. For the holiness I felt when I sat across from him still reverberates in my mind and heart, years later.

If you've ever had God in a box and then released him, you'll understand the absolute wonder this awakens in you. For years, I believed I could tell you pretty much everything there was to know about God. Just look in such-and-such a passage of the Bible. Simple. Then suddenly I found myself in the midst of a group of people who were rousingly in the *midst* of God.

The Jews speak of God in hushed whispers, in rousing discussions, in upthrown hands of perplexity and resignation at all there is yet to discover. They pray as though they can bring God crashing through the roof of the synagogue. They recycle metaphors, expanding God's nature as they do so. They play endlessly with the numerous interpretations and implications of, say, a burning bush and a wrestling angel. After being with them, I always go home amazed. What imagination these Jewish friends of mine have!

After studying and worshiping with the Jews for several months, I began to sense God's presence in a more intense manner in everything around me. The spiritual realities lying beyond the physical world seemed almost tangible. The intense joy I'd feel after a prayer service would remain with me for days.

In addition, because I'd viewed the Bible in such a literal manner as a conservative evangelical, I'd never discovered the much more fascinating, hidden meanings. As I did so, the Bible burst into life—spiritual life.

Because of these things, I wanted to delve deeper, to get to know other Jews and to experience Judaism at different kinds of synagogues. Simchat Torah, the holiday that commemorates the completion of the year-long reading of the Torah, was approaching, and I called Reid to ask for a suggestion as to where I might celebrate it. He said that if I really wanted to immerse myself in the spirit of that particular holiday, I should go to Chabad.

Chabad is an "outreach" synagogue affiliated with the Lubavitchers, a Hasidic sect of Judaism. Most, though not all, Hasidim live in relative isolation from the rest of the world, Jewish and non-Jewish. The Lubavitchers, however, one of the largest Hasidic sects, live among other Jews because it's their mission to help them become more observant. In New York, for instance, they drive several "mitzvah mobiles," stopping by homes of Jews to give them opportunities to perform mitzvot.

The Lubavitchers, like other Hasidim, are considered by many to be ultra-Orthodox because of their strict observance of the law, though in reality, their level of observance doesn't differ that much from many Orthodox Jews. In addition, the Lubavitcher synagogues—or Chabad—are actually more "user-friendly" than are most Orthodox synagogues, with transliteration in their prayer books, some helpful explanations during services, and a low, portable *mechitza* that allows women to touch Torah as it's being carried down the aisles on the Sabbath.

Before the holiday of Simchat Torah arrived, I called Chabad and asked where I should park my car that night because Orthodox Jews do not drive on the Sabbath or holidays, and I could hardly walk the forty miles from my home. I was told that a business across the street allowed the synagogue to use their parking lot, and the high hedges along the street obscured the cars.

Later, I learned that a number of people drive to Chabad, and the Lubavitcher rabbis welcome them with open arms. They're happy that Jews are coming to pray. The Lubavitcher rabbis whom I know are very accepting, tolerant, and kind toward those who are making an effort to become more observant Jews.

But that night I had no idea how kind they were. I even thought they might ask me to leave if they saw I was driving a car. As Mike and I entered the foyer, we noticed that everyone was already inside and we weren't sure what to do. Was it a faux pas in the Jews' eyes for Mike not to wear a *kippah?* Or was it insulting for a non-Jew to wear one? We hadn't even thought about it.

A woman noticed us standing in the foyer and came out to help us. I asked her if Mike should wear a yarmulke, incorrectly pronouncing it just the way it looks: *yar-mulk.* The woman stifled a grin and told me how to pronounce it. She then removed one from a box beside the door, and Mike and I walked quietly into the sanctuary.

Mike had never been inside a synagogue, so he was nervous. In fact, he had threatened to wring my neck if he got pulled into any Jewish dances or circles like the ones I'd described from my visits to other synagogues. I assured him that these were Orthodox Jews, that they would know he was a gentile, and that they certainly wouldn't want him in their Jewish dance circles.

Mike and I took seats on opposite sides of the *mechitza.* The prayer service was in full swing, and a woman handed me a prayer book, pointing to the page number, and helped me follow along.

After the prayer service, Rabbi D., the head rabbi, began calling the men, one by one, to the podium. There, each would give his Hebrew name and then receive a blessing—and a shot of vodka.

It's a custom for most Hasidic Jews to get drunk on Simchat Torah, as this allows one to experience pure, uninhibited joy. In my world up to this point, drunkenness had meant an open door to an anything-goes attitude, an I'll-regret-this-tomorrow feeling. During these services, though, for the Hasidim, it's an opportunity to demonstrate purity even when completely inebriated. And they walk home, as driving isn't allowed on the Sabbath or holidays. In addition, the Hasidim drink alcohol moderately the rest of the year, only getting drunk two times per year as part of religious holidays.

After the last blessing was said, the rabbis removed all the Torahs from the ark, holding them high above their heads, and began circling the room with them. One by one, the men moved into the aisles, joining hands, singing loudly, and dancing. Mike glanced at me with a panicked look in his eyes, just as a man grabbed him and yanked him into the circle. "So I lied," I whispered as he danced around the synagogue in a circle of wildly joyous men.

Again and again the men circled the room, dancing with the Torah scrolls. Occasionally, the Torah would change hands and the man who had been carrying it would stop, throw his hands in the air, and begin a slow, circular hora dance. Rabbi D., his long black beard tucked between a black fedora and black trench coat, captured everyone's attention. With his contagious charisma, he led the dancing and singing and encouraged everyone to get enough vodka. It was Simchat Torah, rejoicing of the Torah, a time to celebrate!

With the prayer service over and the *mechitza* removed, the men and women could mingle, although they weren't allowed to dance together. A couple of women repeatedly tried to get a circle of dancing females going, but most seemed shy or uninterested. So gradually the women moved back to give more room to the men. I was disappointed. The joy in the room was contagious. I didn't want to *watch* anyone dance. I wanted to dance, too!

A small circle of men began to form in the middle of the room. Everyone else gathered around them. One man lifted another onto his shoulders. The circle widened and Rabbi D. did a cartwheel. Others followed suit. The men closest to, but still outside of, the circle were pulled in to do an acrobatic turn or two. Although I was startled when they began tugging on an elderly man, he moved eagerly into the circle, squatted, and did a somersault. Everyone went wild.

At around 10 P.M., Mike and I slipped out. Reid had told us it would be OK to arrive and leave anytime we wanted. "Trust me," he said, "no one will notice, and if they do, they'll never remember the next day. You'll see." We later found out the party had ended between 3 and 4 A.M. The men, including the rabbis, would joke about their hangovers and headaches the next day, but they'd also be up before dawn, reciting their morning prayers in the synagogue.

Although my Baptist church didn't frown on moderate drinking, that was a recent change for me. Until recently, I'd believed that drinking alcohol was immoral, especially because I'd abused it as a teenager. Here, however, the release of inhibitions that alcohol gives was coupled with spiritual joy. The completion of the reading of the Torah, which Simchat Torah celebrates, is a great and happy event, and Jews are supposed to enter into its spirit without holding back. One should be utterly abandoned to the joy of the holiday.

As I left that evening, I was filled with a sense of fun and wonder, but I also realized again how much God is an intricate part of everything in Jewish life—all their activities and thoughts, daily life, and special moments in time. In fact, in Hasidic theology, God can be nothing less.

Like most mystical branches of various religions, the Hasidim believe that everything is an "emanation" of God. God "contracted" himself, and everything—the world around us, mind, spirit, our human bodies—came into being. The idea that God exuberantly permeates everything had begun to create in me, that night, a greater awareness of the vibrant spirit of God in my everyday life.

After the Simchat Torah service, I knew I wanted to become more involved with the Hasidim. I wasn't sure that was possible, but I decided to at least try. Before I left the synagogue, I had noticed a flyer hanging in the foyer and jotted down some information about a study that took place each week in the home of a Lubavitcher rabbi. The next morning, I called and asked if it was OK if I attended. It was.

When Wednesday rolled around, I drove to the rabbi's home (after attending Bible study at my Baptist church) and began the first of many studies with Rabbi G. I'll never forget my first week, when I reached out to shake the hand of a young man who ducked his head and jerked his hand away.[3] Great, I thought, I haven't been here five minutes and already I've offended someone. I was pretty sure they'd move their location the following week and not tell me where they'd gone.

For my first night of study, five men were present. All were intent on learning and practicing a strict observance of Jewish law. For instance, one evening the rabbi discussed whether it was OK to allow someone to interrupt you when you're reciting the *Shema* and, if so, *when* was it OK? Literally hundreds of details surround the recitation of the *Shema*, and we spent part of each Wednesday night sorting through them.

As the weeks wore on, I realized that this was the very reason some people, including many liberal Jews, thought that the

Orthodox were dry and bogged down with irrelevant details about what it means to serve God. Indeed, at first this group seemed to fit my childhood stereotype. But gradually I came to realize that these laws evolved because of a desire to take prayer and obedience seriously. Undoubtedly, I thought, most of us could use a bit of their discipline and the seriousness with which they approach their relationship to God.

I also came to understand that the Hasidim go far beyond a mere adherence to ritual and law. This was driven home to me week after week when, after we'd studied the details of the law, Rabbi G. would open some other Jewish text and plunge us into a world of mystery. I rarely, if ever, heard the rabbi speak of God's wrath or judgment, but I often heard him speak of God's love and grace. And when he spoke of God, he spoke with an intimacy and passion that I knew was genuine. How strange, I thought, that I had once thought of Judaism as a religion that saw God as distant and wrathful.

One evening, Rabbi G. told us an ancient story about a man who had blasphemed and denied God. This man had broken every law and did not keep a single one of the 613 mitzvot, or commands. He had even begun worshiping an idol. Yet with all of this, the rabbi explained, the man wasn't severed from God. Absolutely nothing can break the lifeline between God and man.

I wondered, do we Christians, who talk so easily of the undying, eternal love of God, really believe that our ties with God are this unbreakable?

Another evening, the rabbi was teaching the importance of putting heart and soul into worshiping God. The group listened as he spoke of how essential it is to feel passion toward God rather than simply go through the motions of prayer.

As he taught, two curly brown heads appeared, rounding the corner, and the shifting of our eyes cued the rabbi.

"Mushka!" Rabbi G. said. "Did you let Leah out of the crib?" The girls scampered away, only to return a minute later, the oldest one easing herself onto the table where we were studying. "Mushka!" the rabbi said. "Now you are going to dance on the table?"

With affection and pride showing in his eyes, Rabbi G. excused himself and put the children back to bed. Returning to finish our studies, he raised his voice loudly over the heartbroken wailing in the background until it dissolved into snuffles and, ultimately, silence as the children drifted off to sleep.

"How do we pray the *Shema* with the deepest feeling in our hearts when we pray it three times each day?" the rabbi asked.

"Get Alzheimer's," Boris joked. "Then it's fresh and new every time you say it."

The rabbi ignored him. "You say it like you're counting pearls. Take each one and really look at it and appreciate it. Choose whatever line is most meaningful to you today and feel it with all your heart."

"How do we do it?" Jonathan asked.

The rabbi flipped his hands twice in the air. "How do we do it? How do we do it?" he asked in perplexity.

"I'm not there," Sasha said once when the rabbi was encouraging us to love God intensely at all times.

"That's OK," the rabbi replied. "Neither am I."

Rabbi G. reminded us regularly that God doesn't need angels on earth because he has plenty of them in heaven. He needs humans, Rabbi G. would say. Indeed, even when the men confessed their failures or even their lack of interest in becoming more observant in some areas, Rabbi G. would tell them it was OK and that they should simply make an effort.

As the months wore on, the men (one woman did occasionally attend and, much later, a second woman) became comfortable with me and treated me as they did one another. Besides all I learned, which was a lot, and in addition to the immense amount of depth and mystery that was increasingly infused into my view of God, I also found the men fun and delightful to be around.

During my first year of study with the group, Sasha, one of the regulars, would each week sit in the chair between the rabbi and me and, within a few minutes, would fall into a sound sleep because of his long work hours. Several times during the course of the evening, however, Sasha would awaken and become animated, asking intelligent questions and telling the rabbi how much he appreciated him; he would then fall back asleep.

One night, the rabbi interrupted himself and began addressing Sasha in Russian. The two talked for a few minutes, then Sasha turned and asked me if I had understood what they were talking about. When I told him no, Sasha pinched me on the arm. "That's what the rabbi said he's going to do to me if I don't stay awake."

We laughed as Rabbi G. grinned sheepishly.

A few minutes later, when Sasha again fell asleep, he abruptly jumped up and moved to the opposite end of the table. After that, he often moved back and forth or, more often, would sit at the end of the table to begin with, knowing he'd undoubtedly fall asleep and get pinched. When I asked him teasingly why he had moved, he said he could see the rabbi better, more directly, from the end of the table.

As I look back on the past few years, I'm so grateful I branched out and got to know these men and women who make up only a tiny minority of Jews who live in America. The Hasidim, especially Rabbi G., have deepened my relationship with God in remarkable ways. They've helped me to experience the majesty and mysteries of God, reminded me of the importance of a fervent heart as I seek to become closer to God, and taught me the beauty and importance of ritual. They've also given me a deeper understanding of and love for Judaism.

But one more group particularly enriched my life. About three years ago, my friend Reid recommended that I attend a Jewish service led by a female student rabbi, Hesha Abrams. She and two friends of hers, Joseph and Sherry Schusterman, had organized a *havurah,* or small worship and study group, which initially met once a month at a bank in North Dallas. They were part of a relatively new movement in Judaism called Jewish Renewal.

Jewish Renewal is a branch of Judaism primarily concerned with enriching the spiritual aspect of one's relationship with God. Ideologically, they're liberal, ordaining female rabbis, for instance, rejecting a literal interpretation of scripture, and allowing for many levels of ritual observance. Hesha herself, or Reb Hesha, as we called her, tried to maintain a relatively high level of observance and encouraged members of the *havurah,* called Ruach Torah (literally, spirit of the Torah) to do the same.

My first encounter with the group came when I slipped in late to a service. Although they were in the middle of *Kiddush,* the blessing recited over the wine each Sabbath, Hesha greeted me exuberantly, her striking warmth making me immediately feel comfortable as she invited me into the circle.

The room was bathed only in the warm flickering of the candles. Hesha instructed us to tear a piece of challah, the bread used by Jews on the Sabbath and other occasions, and to feed the person next to us. Hesha held up a salt shaker and asked us what it brought to mind. Several gave answers and, because no one had brought up thirst, I did. Hesha smiled at me. "I sense that you're a woman who thirsts for God," she said.

After *Kiddush,* we turned on the lights and gathered around the tables, opening our prayer books. Hesha chose songs at random, and we alternated singing in English and Hebrew, with a transliteration provided so those who didn't know Hebrew could still sing along. As we sang, Hesha suddenly jumped up, bustled around to my table and hugged me, then returned to her seat and sang with all her heart.

When the singing concluded, we dug into a vegetarian feast and, as we ate, several people came over to talk to me, asking me about my life and my interest in Judaism. Eavesdropping on conversations, I noted that there didn't seem to be any small talk going on but rather deep, personal conversations. Soon Hesha came over and sat next to me. "I see something in your eyes," she said. "Talk to me."

I did.

After the meal, Hesha gave a brief sermon on the Torah portion of the week, then told us to stand and hold hands. "Really feel the hand and the soul of the person standing next to you," Hesha instructed us. "Then go and hug and bless two people." If someone was caught giving a handshake, Hesha would immediately pounce on them. "No! Hug! Hug!" she'd say.

At 11:30 P.M. I finally made my exit, leaving behind several people. No one wanted to leave; I didn't either, but because home was more than a forty-mile drive for me, I had to.

During the next two years, before the *havurah* dissolved due to the *gabbai*'s (rabbinical assistant) health problems and Hesha's schedule (she's a full-time attorney and mother of two teenagers), I would seldom miss a service at Ruach Torah. It was one of the warmest and deepest spiritual experience I've ever had.

In addition to first the monthly then the semimonthly services, we began weekly studies in either Hesha or Joseph's home, and Mike began attending with me. Hesha alternated between speaking to me as if I were Jewish and questioning me about conversion.

"You and Mike have a decision to make," she said to me in front of the group one evening. "Will you make Judaism your primary path to God or a secondary one? If you choose Judaism, *baruch Hashem* (praise the Lord). And if you choose to remain righteous Christians who hang with the Jews, *baruch Hashem*."

In the years Mike and I spent "hanging with them," Hesha and the others treated us as if we were an integral part of the group. Upon her request, I began writing for their newsletter. Hesha even asked me to study so I could help lead the services. "You're a Jew," she sometimes told me, "whether you know it or not."

Once, when I scheduled a party on Friday night (the start of the Jewish Sabbath begins at sundown Friday) and sent Hesha an invitation, she called to gently chide me. "Why did you plan a party on *Shabbat*?" she asked. "Really, why?"

I stuttered to find a reply, realizing that telling her I wasn't Jewish wouldn't suffice. She wouldn't have believed me.

"Well, just make a donation to Israel," she said. "At least that will help."

I did.

One late evening, not long ago, I lay awake reflecting on how deeply I had come to love Judaism and how many exciting experiences I'd had with the Jews. I had, in the past four years, danced with the Torah, received my first traditional Jewish blessing, and learned how to travel through the four mystical levels of scripture. I had munched cookies with an Israeli Hasidic rabbi at the home of another rabbi, danced through the public streets of Dallas with an Orthodox congregation, and watched the final letters of Torah being caressed onto a scroll by a scribe.

Who would have thought it, I smiled to myself? Me, a Baptist living in the Bible Belt, dancing with the Jews.

CHAPTER TWO

Arguing with God

One morning during Sunday school, our teacher asked each of us who our heroes were. "What do you love about them?" Steve asked, "and what do you hate about them?"

Because I was very much into the central teaching of love in Jesus' ministry, I chose Jesus for my hero. So when Steve asked what I loved about him, I replied, "His teaching on love." Steve went on to the next person. "Wait!" I protested. "You forgot to ask me what I hate about him."

Everyone laughed nervously, and someone else started talking. "Really," I said after the person had finished talking, "I want to say what I hate about Jesus."

Silence.

I plunged in. "I hate that Jesus, who's supposed to epitomize love, sounded so harsh with the Jewish leaders. I hate that he singled out the Pharisees so that Christianity, for the past two thousand years, has thought poorly of them and equated a small representation of them with Judaism. [My friend Howard Cohen recently pointed out that even the dictionary equates *Pharisees* with *lack of heart* and a *mere outward show of religion*.] I hate that Jesus called them children of hell, whitewashed tombs, and hypocrites."

At home, I had spent months arguing with God over this matter, eventually beginning to see that Jesus, as an intimate lover of those with whom he shared an ethnicity and genealogy, felt the freedom to grow angry at the ever-present tendency in all of us to lose the heart in our faith. Again, as Howard points out, this was a family squabble among Jews.

Yet to come to this conclusion, I had to argue with God, and this wasn't something that I, as a Christian, felt entirely comfortable with. In the church, we're often taught that anger toward God is inappropriate and shows a lack of respect. "God said it; I believe it; that settles it," says a popular cliché, and it's one that, in the past, you could have stamped on my forehead.

The Jews, however, are not only comfortable arguing with God, they relish it! "We argue with God," said one woman at Reid's study group. "He always wins, but we still argue!" Indeed, Jacob's namesake, Yisra-El (Israel), means "struggle with God." He wrestled with the angel, and the Jews have followed suit ever since—except that they're in the ring with God himself.

Anthropologist and author Barbara Myerhoff, who did an ethnography of a Jewish retirement home, wrote of one woman's comments:

> After the Day of Judgment, all the Jews will . . . spend eternity studying Torah together, at last arguing with the Lord Himself about the right interpretation of His Law. This is the Jew's idea of Paradise. Do we have angels peacefully riding on clouds with their harps playing. . . . No, we have a big debate with God, a pilpul in the sky.[1]

What a wonderful intimacy the Jews have with God! We don't speak like this to one who merely makes us shake in fear, I've learned, or to an impersonal Being whom we serve with heartless rituals and laws. We speak like this to someone to whom we feel close.

Elie Wiesel tells of a time when the Shpoler rebbe, Rabbi Leib (also known as the Zeide) became upset at God after a famine began to devastate his land. Many great Hasidic masters had written the rebbe and begged him to use his powers to "change the heavenly decrees and their heavy curses," and so the rebbe, with a plan in mind, invited ten spiritual giants to come and visit him as soon as possible.

When the ten men arrived, the rebbe sat them down and announced that he intended to bring suit against the "Blessed Name . . . seeking judgment according to the law of the Torah." The tribunal who would try God would be in session, he said, for three days.

The rebbe's beadle (his personal assistant) was the only one allowed to come near the gathering, and he left an eyewitness account of the proceedings. "'I alone was allowed to enter. . . . But as soon as I crossed the threshold, an unknown anguish took hold of me—so powerful I could not breathe. . . .'"

For three days, the tribunal brought out Torah, Talmud, dozens of texts, commentaries, rabbinical decrees, and decisions as evidence of God's guilt against his people. "The court," writes Wiesel, "deliberated without fear or prejudice, examining the problem from all angles, weighing all arguments."

On the fourth day, the ten judges seated themselves at the table with the rebbe, and the beadle announced that the tribunal was in session. "In the name of all the feeble women and all the starving children," exclaimed the rebbe, "I lodge a complaint against Him who could and should feed them and help them but does not. He who gave us the Torah is obliged to respect its law. And the law enjoins the Master to take care of his servants."

The rebbe, the beadle remembered, was covered with sweat, his eyes burned, and his body trembled. Then the judges "cried out as with a single voice: 'The tribunal sides with Rabbi Leib, son of Rachel. We decree that it behooves God blessed be He to feed the children and their mothers.'"

God had been tried in a Jewish court of law and had been found guilty.

"Rebbe Leib," says Wiesel, "was on the side of man, defending him even against God: 'Lord, You are unjust. You filled books with hell and hearts with desire; is it surprising then that man permits himself to be seduced by evil? Now, if it were the other way around. . . .'"

The rebbe also stood with hands on hips, telling God that if he thought he'd draw anyone close to him by making them suffer, he had another thought coming. "I, Leib, son of Rachel, swear to You that You will not succeed," he said. "So why try?"[2]

Another story is told by Lawrence Kushner in which, during the holiday of Yom Kippur, when all sins are confessed and forgiven by God, Rabbi Levi Yitzhak of Berditchev noticed that one of his most devout members, a tailor, was absent. So the rabbi left the synagogue and went to the man's home where he found him sitting at the table with a piece of paper.

When the rabbi questioned him, the tailor said he was listing his sins. Then, on the other side of the paper, he was listing God's. The tailor showed the rabbi the list. For every sin he had committed, he said, God had committed one, too. So after finishing his list, he had told God, "Look, we each have the same number of sins. If you let me off, I'll let You off!"

As soon as the rabbi heard this, he scolded the tailor angrily. "You fool!" he said. "You had Him and you let Him go!"[3]

And here is still another tale, this time from Rabbi Gordis. In a famous Talmudic story, Rabbi Eliezer disagrees with the other sages about whether a certain oven is permissible for use. Rabbi Eliezer introduces every imaginable argument to convince the sages that it is, but they disagree. Finally, he resorts to miracles to try and persuade them.

"If the law agrees with me," says Rabbi Eliezer, "let this carob tree prove it!" Suddenly, the tree moves a hundred cubits, but the sages dismiss the miracle, saying a moving tree proves nothing. The rabbi tries again. "If the law agrees with me," he says, "let the stream of water prove it!" In response, the water begins flowing backwards! However, the sages are nonplused, arguing that this, too, is little proof.

A third time, Rabbi Eliezer attempts to get the sages to agree with him. If he is right, he declares, let the walls of the schoolhouse confirm it; with that, the walls begin to lean. (The Talmud notes that the walls, at the time of writing, still stood in a tilt in honor of Rabbi Eliezer.) Still, the sages aren't moved to change their minds.

The rabbi tries one last miracle, saying that the oven's permissibility would be affirmed by God himself, and immediately a voice from heaven reprimands the sages, asking them why they are disputing Rabbi Eliezer—that the law is, indeed, on his side.

This is too much. One of the sages, Rabbi Joshua, stands up and says that the Torah was given long ago at Mount Sinai and that they will pay no attention to a Heavenly Voice. The Torah, he says, teaches that one should follow the ruling of the majority and, in this case, Rabbi Eliezer was standing alone.

When God hears this, he begins laughing with pleasure. "My children have defeated Me!" God says. "My children have defeated Me!"[4]

God has been backed into a corner by his people—and is utterly delighted!

For me, these aren't merely intriguing stories, though they *are* that; they're stories that teach me about relationship, that intimacy calls for holding another to a sense of responsibility and involvement. If God feels distant and unconcerned, then we should argue with him! We should feel free to let him know we're angry and hurt, honestly expressing our feelings and thoughts. This, I've learned in part from the Jews, is what relationship is all about, and we can have it with God.

Undoubtedly, we're all familiar with the story of Moses coming blissfully off Mount Sinai, fresh from an encounter with God, only to discover that the Hebrews had grown tired of waiting and had crafted a golden calf to worship in place of God. The Bible states that God is furious. "I have seen this people," God says to Moses, "how stiff-necked they are. Now let me alone, so that my wrath may burn hot against them and I may consume them."

Moses, however, begs God to turn back his anger. He reminds God of his love for his people, pointing out that the Egyptians would mock him if he destroyed Israel. Asking God to change his mind, Moses brings up the names of Abraham, Isaac, and Jacob and reminds God of the promises made to them. Moses was apparently successful in his intercession, for scripture says, God "reconsidered regarding the evil that He declared He would do to His people" (Exodus 32:14).

As a Christian, I've always intellectualized this passage, dismissing it as ridiculous to think that a man, Moses, changed God's mind. In truth, few Jews would take it literally, either. But the point is, though most Jews don't think man can literally change God's mind, neither do they dismiss this passage.

Although I've never studied this particular scripture with any group of Jews, I imagine a discussion would go something like this: "Moses argues with God! He backs God into a corner, reminds him of his promises. Moses is on man's side because man needs to be defended and protected. Did God actually change his mind? Irrelevant question! Who knows about God? Who knows about the paradox of scripture? The point is—we argue! We call God into account. We pray because . . . who knows what can happen?"

I love this approach to scripture and to God. For so many years, I was only concerned with a purely literal approach to the Bible. I wanted to get past these passages as quickly as possible, knowing there was no good, logical explanation that would leave the Bible intact as the inerrant Word of God. I believed faith was superior to our intellect, so I'd simply dismiss any discussion on troubling passages such as these.

As I began my spiritual journey away from the strictest forms of evangelicalism, however, I took an equally unsatisfying approach, believing that as a book written by fallible men, certain passages in the Bible were unreliable and irrelevant. Moses may have prayed, I reasoned, but he certainly didn't change God's mind. What else to do but skim past another passage, only this time because I *did* trust my intellect and felt I had to dismiss the story as meaningless.

The Jewish way with scripture bypasses both methods of encounter with biblical stories. Some Jews, particularly the Orthodox, may indeed take the passage literally (although they'll probably have years of discussion about it and thousands of inter- pretations), but virtually all will go beyond the logical problems it creates and find some surprising, hidden, often mysterious mean- ing. We don't know about God, they might say, but we know about Moses arguing with God.

I've often wondered at how Christianity might become more attractive if we were allowed to argue with God in this way. In the past, when I've faced difficulties and painful situations, I've sometimes been told by Christians to "just have faith." And of course, that *is* the goal. But we can better reach it after we've stated our case, told God what's on our minds, and put him "on trial" for the pain in our hearts and in the world.

At the heart of Judaism and thus another answer to the question, Who are the Jews? is the emphasis on ritual as a path to entering God's presence. One of the most beautiful of these involves the structure of the Jewish prayer service. Whether it's a three-hour Orthodox service conducted entirely in Hebrew or a considerably shorter, liberal Reform service, each part of the service is ritualized and deeply symbolic. Attending synagogue, for me, has been an incredibly worshipful experience.

Except for a short sermon, a Jewish service simply consists of prayer, and the entire congregation participates. When I attend, I alternate reading the prayers silently in English and struggling along with the transliteration. When I'm doing the latter, even though I don't understand the meaning of the words, I absorb the worshipful atmosphere. Jews believe the holiness of the Hebrew language affects the worshiper whether or not he or she understands on an intellectual level.

Years ago, I thought reading prayers indicated sterility and lack of heart. How silly this was. Reading prayers has allowed me a deeper concentration because I'm engaging my sense of sight as well as my sense of hearing. The prayers in the Jewish prayer book are magnificent, many of them ancient or written by those who have had powerful experiences with God. Reading them allows me to pick up on the spiritual energy of the one who wrote it, usually a great tzaddik (saint) or a poet, such as David.

A force is present in many of these prayers that's often far more potent than a spontaneous prayer offered off the top of one's head. In addition, bending over a prayer book, trying to read with *kavanah* (intent) and heart takes my thoughts and eyes off others and thus allows me to enter into personal interaction with God.

The reverence of the Jews for God is thoroughly evident during a prayer service. *"Kadosh, kadosh, kadosh,"* I say with the Jews ("Holy, holy, holy"). At the sound of each word, we rise onto our toes, symbolizing the angels as they flow back and forth before the throne of God. *"Baruch ata Adonai"* ("Blessed is the Eternal"). We bend our knees, then bow forward.

Later, as the ark is opened, the *Aleinu* prayer is recited: "We bow and prostrate ourselves in gratitude before the Sovereign Ruler of the world, the Holy, Blessed One." Together, we bow low. When I'm with the Jews, I am always symbolically prostrating myself before a holy and loving God.

Observant Jews recite specific prayers three times a day at ritually designated times. Most Orthodox Jewish men put on tefillin (phylacteries) and tallit (prayer shawls) and pray each morning at sunrise at the synagogue. Other Jews may pray at home. Regardless of how they do it, though, many Jews begin and end their day with a remembrance of God. This has been a lovely lesson for me.

Keeping kosher is also important to most Jews, though again, levels of observance depend on ideology. Orthodox Jews have separate utensils and often separate refrigerators for dairy products and meat.[5] *Shochet*s are special butchers who follow levitical guidelines for slaughtering, and rabbis are present to ensure it's done properly.

Keeping kosher has deep meaning for a Jew, and understanding this has helped me go beyond a superficial reading of certain passages in the Bible. One Jewish friend explains that all forbidden animals have some quality about them that we should avoid spiritually. Birds of prey, for instance, are forbidden in order to teach us that we shouldn't prey on others.

The law also commands Jews to eat only animals that have a split hoof and chew the cud. Rabbi G. says that the split hoof represents an ability to separate the godly from the animalistic, while chewing the cud symbolizes study and internal absorption. Both are necessary.

Ritual in general brings people together and unites them emotionally, says Tom Driver in *The Magic of Ritual*. It provides rich symbolism, memorializes liberating events, and effects transformation. Ritual uses these symbols to "invoke, to address, to affect, even to manipulate, one or another unseen power." To lose ritual, writes Driver, is to lose one's way.[6]

My friend Hesha says to think of ritual as an access code to the divine. The focus, though, she quickly adds, is on the divine, not the access code. "It's like accessing the Internet," she explains. "Some people just want to do e-mail, but others want to really get into the 'net,' and so they need a number of access codes." Ritual, she says, is "accessing the spiritual Internet."

Because I grew up in a religious denomination that places little importance on ritual, I've been captivated by the richness of this aspect of Judaism. The symbolic aspects of ritual might be compared to storytelling, and because our minds are hard-wired to absorb the messages in stories more easily than in abstract ideas and principles, ritual can provide a more meaningful worship and prayer experience.

When I worship with the Jews, for instance, the physical act of bowing or bending my knees when certain phrases are recited reminds me that I'm addressing, that I'm in the presence of, a holy

Being. As I watch Sabbath candles being lit, I feel the warmth and the changing atmosphere as the work week passes into a period of rest and holiness. Ritual, when done mindfully, often intensifies and heightens spiritual awareness.

Enmeshed in ritual and close to the heart of the Jew is the Sabbath—a day imbued with mystery and holiness, a day unlike all others, which is welcomed, permeated throughout, and departs in ritual.

A couple of years ago, I decided to drive to Colorado from Texas to attend a Torah retreat. I knew absolutely nothing about the community, had never been to an intensive Jewish study retreat, and had no idea if I'd be accepted or welcomed.

The retreat turned out to be hosted by a small community of men and women trying to follow the beliefs and practices of the Hasidim, though without the dress or separation that many Hasidic communities practice. The retreat was led by a Hasidic rabbi from Israel, a founder and leader of a yeshiva (Jewish seminary) affiliated with the Breslover sect of Hasidim, and another Hasidic rabbi from New York, who was affiliated with the Hasidic branch called the Viznitzers.

I was welcomed and included throughout the week. In fact, one of the women in the community welcomed me into her home, giving me a room and a key and assuring me that I should feel at home while staying with her. Although I was usually around only to sleep, occasionally she'd catch me and invite me to the kitchen, and we'd share snacks and long conversations. The entire week turned out to be one of the most incredible experiences of my life.

At the conclusion of the retreat, as the Sabbath drew near, a young woman came over to me and quietly asked if I'd like to light the Sabbath candles with her. Although she knew I wasn't Jewish, she wanted me to feel a part of the group. As Rachel recited the appropriate blessings, we waved our arms inward, from the flame to our hearts, welcoming the Sabbath.

Baruch ata Adonai
Eloheinu melech ha-olam
asher ķidshanu b'mitzvotav
v'tzivanu l'hadliķ ner shel
Shabbat.

"Blessed art Thou, Lord our God, King of the universe who has sanctified us with His commandments and ordained that we kindle the Sabbath light."

I watched Rachel for a few moments, enthralled by the peaceful expression that spread over her face, then I closed my eyes and breathed in the joy and rest that Sabbath brings.

Several years back, I had studied Abraham Joshua Heschel's classic work on the Sabbath with Reid's group. Heschel taught that the Sabbath had been created by God with a special substance—*menuha*—and that this filled it with an inexplicable quality of rest and joy and holiness.

"The Sabbaths are our great cathedrals," Heschel writes. "It is a day . . . to turn from the results of creation to the mystery of creation; from the world of creation to the creation of the world." There is an "essence" to the day itself. Heschel points out that Sabbath isn't a day to recover from the week; it's a day to celebrate life, a "climax of living." Fasting, mourning, and demonstrations of grief are forbidden on the Sabbath, he adds.[7]

I read somewhere that the Hasidic tradition teaches that the Sabbath should never end without making love. It is a day of celebration, praise, and joy, not just spiritually but holistically. The Sabbath is for comfort and pleasure.

As a Christian, I'd never paid much attention to the Sabbath. I attended church on Sunday (the Christian Sabbath) and gave little thought to how I spent the remainder of the day. Certainly I'd never regarded it as a day with a distinctive "essence." Yet after studying Heschel's work, I began to feel a presence about the Jewish holy day. There seemed to be something truly sacred about it.

My week in Colorado was the first time I'd had the privilege of celebrating the Jewish Sabbath in its entirety. After the Friday evening service, the *mechitza* that separates men and women in Orthodox services came down, and the men and women began dancing exuberantly in separate circles. Uninhibited joy bounded across the room. Someone grabbed me and pulled me into the center of the circle. We joined hands and twirled, faster and faster, as everyone danced around us, clapping their hands and singing.

The Sabbath meal, shared after the Saturday morning Torah service, is also an important and joyful Sabbath ritual. Many in the Orthodox community host a Sabbath meal in their home, inviting several members of their synagogue. If visitors show up, they'll also be invited to one of the homes. In keeping with the laws of Sabbath, the meal is prepared Friday afternoon before sunset and the beginning of the Sabbath.

At the Colorado retreat, following the Torah service on Saturday morning, everyone cleared the rented room of prayer books and tallit and began to set up long tables, covering them with white tablecloths. Men and women bustled around in the kitchen, moving plates of rice, buffalo meat, and tzimmes (a carrot dish) through an assembly line of hands. Someone began a familiar

Jewish chorus, and dozens of voices joined in. The atmosphere became almost rambunctious in its light-heartedness and volume.

In the center of the room, a young Hasid began pounding a table in a melodic rhythm. Two others began a table-pounding accompaniment. Dancing broke out. The Hasidic rabbi from Israel joined in. The shy Hasidic rabbi from New York stood in a corner watching, his face filled with the happy glow of Sabbath joy.

Soon the ceremonial washing of hands began. About 150 local Jews joined us for the meal, though only about 30 attended the week-long retreat, and the line snaked across the room and into the kitchen. Like the others, I cupped water and dashed it onto my left hand, then my right. I emerged from the kitchen and joined the throngs of people still singing at the tops of their voices, bouncing one another on their knees, banging tables, throwing their hands in the air.

This was utterly new for me. I could remember leisurely afternoon drives and family dinners on the Christian Sabbath but nothing that infused the day with such honor, ritual, and holiness. Later I learned that washing the hands imitates, in this instance, the ritual handwashing performed by the *kohen* (priests) before they ate the consecrated food. In all cases, however, the main purpose of ritual handwashing is to "become holy." How lovely, I thought, to enact a ritual that makes this time of eating together a holy act.

As we sang, I searched the room for Rivka, a middle-aged woman who had become my guardian during the week. Earlier, when an Orthodox rabbi had approached me to ask about "my story" (word had apparently circulated that I was a non-Jew interested in Judaism), Rivka appeared out of nowhere, patting me on the back.

"Are you leaving?" I had asked her.

"No, I'm just patting," she said. Then, whispering in my ear, she added, "I'm just letting the rabbi know we love and accept you."

So it was Rivka I often sought out when I wasn't sure what to do and now, after the ceremonial handwashing, I slipped into a seat beside her and whispered a question. Her eyes grew big, and she pursed her lips together in exaggerated fashion. I realized I wasn't supposed to speak but didn't know why.

Suddenly, the rabbi raised his hands and the room began to grow still. He raised a glistening butcher knife in his hand and whacked the challah vigorously, cutting through three paper table-cloths and flinging crumbs six feet in every direction. The room erupted, and great bowls of food were passed from table to table. Rivka explained that Orthodox Jews don't speak between the time of handwashing and breaking challah, and I later learned that when the priests performed their rituals, they did so in complete silence for the sake of concentration.

My talking during this ritual wasn't the only faux pas I'd made. In fact, they'd pretty much become a way of life for me. That morning, for instance, I had stashed my purse in a corner of the Masonic Lodge where we were meeting when I suddenly remembered that Orthodox Jews don't carry anything on the Sabbath. As the food was passed around, however, I snuck back to my purse and retrieved a few quarters to purchase a Coke from the machine. When Rivka saw me, she grabbed my arm and became very serious. "Put that money away!" she said. "Orthodox Jews don't buy things on Shabbos. We don't even want to see money on Shabbos."

She was so intense that I sat down and stuck the money under my leg. "I realize you aren't a Jew, but let's be safe," she said. Then her voice turned to a whisper and she looked around conspiratorially. "If you have to have a Coke, then sneak down to the store and buy one later." Rivka wiggled into a seat beside me. "If I weren't already a Jew," she sighed, "I don't know if I'd become one. It's so hard. It's so hard to be a Jew."

Still another faux pas had occurred not too many months earlier, when I had pulled out my journal at a Jewish Renewal Sabbath service in order to take notes on the sermon. "Put that away!" Hesha had said, slapping my hands. "Jews aren't supposed to write on *Shabbat*." (Hesha has always treated me as if I were Jewish, which tickles and delights me.)

Of course, the Jews could also turn the tables on me. At still another service, this time at a Traditional synagogue (Orthodox without the *mechitza*), I had run from my car to the door of the shul in a blinding rainstorm, thinking it disrespectful to carry an umbrella. Even though my sprint was short, by the time I flung open the door of the synagogue, I was soaked to the bone, my hair a dripping mess.

Inside, several people were setting their umbrellas in the foyer. When I questioned a friend, she laughed. "Jews don't like to get wet," she said.

I had no idea whether the Orthodox community in Boulder would have agreed, but I wasn't taking any chances. After the money incident, I put away my purse and my umbrella and, when I was unsure about it, my voice.

After the Sabbath festivities were over and we had all pitched in to clean up, I headed back to my room, opened a window, and set a fan nearby to circulate the warm air. I reached for my journal, then set it down again. Instead, I gazed out the window, meditating on the special holiness with which the Jews regard this day. I decided not to write anything down, as would have been my usual custom. Instead, I closed my eyes and concentrated on the breeze caressing my face. I fell asleep, embraced in the memories of the day.

CHAPTER THREE

Dancing with the Torah

It's 3:30 in the morning when I slip into a Conservative synagogue. A lively study is taking place—at least by those who are still awake. Several people are sitting straight up in their chairs, sound asleep. A couple of others mosey over to the snack table to get a bowl of protein-filled peanuts, a cup of coffee, or a plate of sweets—whatever will keep them awake for a few more hours.

It's the festival of Shavuot—the anniversary of the day on which Moses is believed to have received Torah on Mount Sinai. In the mystical tradition of Judaism, Moses spent three periods consisting of forty days each on Mount Sinai. During the first forty days, he received the entire Torah. During the second forty days, he received the oral law, and during the final forty days, he received the mystical teachings, or kabbalah.

Many Jews, mostly the Orthodox and Conservative, follow the tradition to stay up all night studying. I've heard that in Israel, where synagogues are in close proximity to one another, some Jews walk from one synagogue to another (Orthodox Jews don't drive on holidays), so I've decided, in following tradition, to synagogue-hop (though I'm definitely driving!). My friend Karen Prager and I decide to begin the evening at her synagogue, Temple Emanu-El, which is Reform.

After hanging out at the snack table for a while, we all take our seats and Rabbi Mark Kaiserman makes the tongue-in-cheek announcement that we're going to read the entire Torah. He hands each of us a slip of paper with a *parsha,* or Torah portion, high-lighted. We're to read our portion, choose a verse that particularly speaks to us, then, when we're all finished, stand one by one and read the verses in order, beginning with the *parsha* that includes Genesis 1 and ending with the one that includes the final chapter of Deuteronomy.

We're off. *"Parsha Bereishis,"* calls out Rabbi Kaiserman. Someone stands and reads, "HASHEM God called out to the man and said to him, 'Where are you?'" *"Parsha Noach,"* says Rabbi Kaiserman, and someone else reads, "And as for Me, behold, I establish My covenant with you and with your offspring after you."

One person stands up and sings her verse, and Karen leans over and whispers to me, "It's wild tonight!" As we finish the first four books of Torah and launch into Deuteronomy, one man stands to read what's supposed to be his verse, but a dozen people notice that he's reading from Genesis. Two of them, in fact, know which chapter he's reading from.

It's just the kind of moment Rabbi Kaiserman loves—an opportunity to tease someone. "Stop!" he says. "Everyone please take a moment to check your Bible. The book of Genesis is *not* included in the book of Deuteronomy. If everyone will stop for a moment's reflection, they'll realize that we've long since left the book of Genesis and are now in the book of *Deuteronomy.* Please do stay away from the wine table, and let's continue reading."

"It's wild tonight," whispers Karen.

When we're finished reading Torah, Marc Kivel leads a short study from the book of Ruth—the biblical book traditionally read on Shavuot. He hands out a sheet of paper with verses from Ruth, other scriptures that illuminate these verses, Talmudic quotes, midrash, rabbinical comments, ancient Jewish philosophers' insights, and at least one modern Jewish author. One verse into the study, fifteen hands shoot up. Comments and debates begin. The three rabbis in the room jump in. It's going to be a typical night of study with a group of Jews.

At midnight the study winds to a close. Everyone goes home to sleep, except for Karen and me. With the back streets of Dallas already deserted, we head for Rabbi G.'s—the Hasidic rabbi with whom I studied regularly for several years. We climb the flight of stairs and are greeted enthusiastically by the rabbi and the four people attending his study. "Where have you been studying tonight?" they ask, and someone jokingly wants to know if we've been studying the Buddha. They ask us how long we plan to stay up studying.

"I'm here for as long as you are," I reply.

Rabbi G. is delighted. "She's challenging us!" he says.

Karen, my liberal feminist friend, takes a seat across from a woman who will walk home alone at 2:30 A.M., refusing a ride from me because it's a Jewish holiday. Plastic liters of Coke sit alongside cinnamon rolls scattered along the table. I haven't seen the group in a few months, and the study comes to an abrupt halt so everyone can ask where I've been, what I've been doing, how I am. They've missed me, they say. My liberal Jewish friends shake their heads in amazement over this relationship, but to me it's become a comfortable, trusting friendship. I like them and they like me.

Rabbi G. plunges into a Talmudic text, then veers off into ancient, mystical stories. He tells us of a period in time when the world was so full of Hashem's light, before wickedness increased, that a person's senses mingled together, causing each sense to experience God with the fullness of all the others. There was no echo, he says, because each breath and whisper of wind was the voice of God, and the trees and all of nature absorbed that voice.

The rabbi pauses to tell us, wondrously, that no one can reach the end of Torah study. There are ten thousand levels, he says, and each of these levels contains ten thousand more.

"What is the difference between a portrait and a photograph?" Rabbi G. suddenly asks. Everyone offers an answer, and Sasha replies that the portrait allows more imagination. Rabbi G. is thrilled. "Sasha is awake tonight!" he says. (Sasha is the man the rabbi sometimes threatens to pinch so he'll remain awake while we're studying.)

"A picture captures the same detail each time, but with portraits, each is individualized," Rabbi G. says, adding that we are God's portraits.

At Chabad, at least in the Dallas area, it's tradition to teach only about half the night, so around 2:30 A.M. Rabbi G. begins wrapping things up. Karen goes home, but I head for the next synagogue—a Traditional one. When I arrive, small groups are gathered around several tables, engaged in raucous discussion. I sit with a group of teenagers led by a friend, David Abrams, and listen. It's been less than a year since the 9/11 tragedy, and the teens are discussing terrorism, leaning over the table, talking over one another, struggling to deal with what, to them, as Jews, is an intensely personal issue.

Because I'm anxious to get to another study, I only stay a few minutes, then drive several more miles to another synagogue. I had begun my evening with the Reform, moved to the Hasidim, dropped in on the Traditional, and was now headed to a Conservative synagogue.

At Shearith Israel, I'm delighted to discover that one of the guest rabbis, David Stein, an outstanding and engaging teacher, is one who had taught a ten-week Talmud class I'd attended the year before. Although each synagogue follows tradition, reading and studying the book of Ruth for Shavuot, each takes a different, interesting approach.

One of Rabbi Stein's topics is whether Ruth's conversion to Judaism was from a genuine love of Israel's God, whether her devotion primarily extended to her mother-in-law, or whether it was a mix of both. This generates discussion of whether modern conversions brought on by love of another human being are as sincere as those coming from a simple love of Judaism. Rabbi Stein, having participated in conversions from both motives, tells us that he's come to believe that conversion for the sake of a lover is just as deep and sincere as any other.

As with any discussion of the book of Ruth, the question comes up whether she and Boaz had made love in the field. Although I'd heard the discussion many times, including whether "uncovering the feet" was a euphemism for uncovering something more "private," Rabbi Stein provided a lengthier explanation.

The word used for "his legs" is *margelotav,* which is close to the word *margeliotav*—the latter meaning "pearls" and being the word chosen by the writer. "His jewels!" adds someone in the congregation, and everyone laughs. Rabbi Stein explains that the word *margelotav* certainly was known to the writer, so there was obviously some play on the word, but what, we aren't sure. Furthermore, Rabbi Stein points out that Boaz kept Ruth with him all night, then "slipped her out" in the morning. He also gave her far more grain than was necessary or typical. "Obviously, the woman was hot," Rabbi Stein adds.

However, the rabbi concludes that whatever went on at the threshing floor, it probably wasn't sexual intercourse. He points out that in chapter four, for instance, the writer of Ruth tells us that it wasn't until after Boaz had gone through the proper channels, offering Ruth to the next of kin, that he finally "took [her] and she became his wife; and he came to her."

The next rabbi, Elon Sunshine, hands out a sheet of paper with the worshipful Psalm 148 printed on it. I carefully read through it with the group but wasn't prepared for the mesmerizing discussion that lasted for nearly an hour, until the rabbi had to bring it to a close.

Here's the psalm:

Hallelujah.
Praise the LORD from the heavens;
    praise Him on high.
Praise Him, all his angels,
    praise Him, all his hosts.
Praise Him, sun and moon,
    praise Him, all bright stars.
Praise Him, highest heavens,
    and you waters that are above the heavens.
Let them praise the name of the LORD,
    for it was He who commanded that they be created.
He made them endure forever,
    establishing an order that shall never change.
Praise the LORD, O you who are on earth,
    all sea monsters and ocean depths,
    fire and hail, snow and smoke,
    storm that executes His command,
    all mountains and hills,

all fruit trees and cedars,
    all wild and tamed beasts,
    creeping things and winged birds,
    all kings and peoples of the earth,
    all princes of the earth and its judges,
    youths and maidens alike,
    old and young together.
Let them praise the name of the LORD,
    for His name, His alone, is sublime;
    His splendor covers heaven and earth.
He has exalted the horn of His people
    for the glory of all His faithful ones,
    Israel, the people close to Him.
    Hallelujah.

The moment Rabbi Sunshine finishes reading the psalm, everyone jumps in. "It reflects the order of creation from the sun and moon to animals," one man says. "Everything's individualized in the beginning, then it all comes together toward the middle," says another. And a third person: "Every individual thing and animal and person is commanded individually to praise, then suddenly there is one single command to everything and everyone to praise. That's an indication that we progress from separateness to unity."

"Maybe praise isn't the best word," adds one man. "I have a problem with inanimate objects praising. What about showing praise?"

"Too passive for me," replies the rabbi. "This is an active chapter. So what about the idea that as each object fulfills its purpose—the water gushes, trees blossom, fire burns, wind flows and cools—it's praising." Everyone loves that.

"I get the picture of an orchestra," says one man. "Each object and animal and person has its own melody but all come together in a symphony of praise."

"Notice the culmination: young and old, men and women. Egalitarian."

"I don't like this scripture. It sounds like God is an egoist, a Being who has to be praised or he gets angry at us."

"No, it's relationship," replies a rabbi sitting with the congregation. "What is God said to keep in his tefillin? Israel. He praises humankind. We praise him. It's a lover's exchange."

On and on they go. Endlessly. I remember Rabbi G.'s comment earlier in the evening that Torah has ten thousand levels and that each level has ten thousand levels within it. Listening to the Jews debate and discuss makes me believe it. Their insights are rich and deep. I feel I could listen to them for days without eating or sleeping.

As sunlight begins to peek through the window, though, the study draws to a close. As we walk to chapel for the morning service, the men talk of having been in Jerusalem on this holiday. "It's the most incredible experience," one of them says. "Every synagogue has been packed the entire evening, then, as day breaks, literally thousands and thousands of men, women, and children flood the streets, rushing toward the Wall to pray."

The image that rises to my mind enthralls me. Years back, a Jewish friend had gently tried to stem some of my enthusiasm, saying that too much romanticizing when I wrote of the Jews might make someone uncomfortable. But to me, the Jews and Judaism are unbelievably romantic. I can't help gushing. Now, as the Jews don their beautifully embroidered tallit, swaying gently as they chant their prayers, I close my eyes and embrace the atmosphere with my whole heart and soul. I've been up the entire night and have an hour's drive home, but falling asleep during the drive isn't even a remote possibility. I'm pumped spiritually, and the love and joy I feel courses through my body, making me feel intensely alive—and awake.

How the Jews love to study! A couple of years earlier, Hesha had asked me to write about our Shavuot celebration for Ruach Torah's newsletter. I wrote that we had spent the evening around a table piled high with dozens and dozens of books. "Study isn't just a Jewish tradition," I had written. "It's the Jewish condition."

"I love it! I love it!" exclaimed Hesha to the newsletter's editor. "Print it just as it is!"

Study is, first and foremost, a sacred command from God. Writes Rabbi Binyomin Menachem Adilman, "HASHEM loves the Torah learning of Klal Yisroel so much, that he decreed . . . that in order that a Jew should continue learning with enthusiasm his whole life, one should learn and then forget, and then learn it all over again!!"[1]

Tales of what pious Jews have done as they've sought to immerse themselves in study are endless and mind-boggling. Joshua Hammer writes that one rabbi who suffered excruciating pain from an inoperable disk malformation in his neck would use a weighted pulley to relieve pressure so he could study each day from 9 A.M. to midnight.[2] Although few are this devoted to study, study is certainly inseparable from Jewishness. Many Hasidic and Orthodox masters left their families for long periods of time in order to devote themselves without distraction—or even breaks—to study.

On a boy's first day of Hebrew school, as he began to learn the Hebrew alphabet, it was once a custom for the teacher to show him his first letter—*aleph*—then place a drop of honey on his tongue.

"How does that taste?" the teacher would ask.

"Sweet," the student would reply.

"Study of the law," the teacher would say, "is sweeter."

It didn't take many hours of studying with the Jews for me to understand this. In grade school, I had memorized several verses out of the familiar Psalm 119, which I still remember. The King James version, from which we memorized, poetically translates them: "Thy Word is a lamp unto my feet, and a light unto my path," reads verse 105, and in verse 11, "Thy word have I hid in mine heart, that I might not sin against thee."

As I grew up, I loved this psalm and memorized other verses within it, but after I began studying with the Jews, Psalm 119 took on an even more profound meaning. Because Jewish study is so imaginative and playful, I rarely felt as though I was learning with my intellect alone. Learning "about" God meant discovering new ways to *experience* God. This, I began to understand, is why the law is so sweet to the Jews and why David could write so lovingly and enthusiastically about it; a more expansive knowledge of the law equaled a more powerful and immeasurable encounter with God.

In addition to the Bible, though, Jews carefully study other texts as well. In yeshiva (seminary) training, for instance, knowledge of Talmud, the source of Jewish law, is considered of utmost importance. The Talmud explains and expands the Torah, and Jews use it, with varying degrees of strictness, to aid their understanding and application of Torah.

Talmud is the combination of Mishnah and Gemara. Mishnah is the Oral Torah, which some say was given by God, along with the written Torah and the mystical writings, to Moses on Mount Sinai. The Oral Torah was eventually written down out of fear it would be lost.

The Gemara is a commentary on the Mishnah. It offers glosses of the fascinating stories, folk wisdom, and midrashim (parables) and endless arguments of the sages, scholars, and rabbis in which they quote the authoritative Mishnah, Torah, and some important oral sources outside the Mishnah.

When I first began ordering volumes of Talmud and reading through them, I was reprimanded by virtually every Jewish friend I have. "Talmud isn't for reading," said Rabbi G. "It's for study." Others discouraged me from tackling it alone, explaining that Talmud was best studied with a group.

Indeed, the Jewish way is to study in small groups or with a partner. Yeshiva libraries aren't quiet places with divided coves for individual study. They are noisy. They're designed so two heads bent over a book can eavesdrop on the two heads next to them, encouraging new avenues for discussion. The Torah retreat that I attended in Colorado was set up to simulate this study environment and, at Ruach Torah, we were each assigned a permanent study partner. I learned firsthand how enriching this kind of study is.

Taking Talmud lightly—merely reading it—is understandably insulting to those who have spent years mastering tiny portions of it. Rabbi Stein, for instance, explained to us during our introductory Talmud classes that he had spent seven years of rabbinical school mastering seventy-five pages of it.

Rabbi G. always had fascinating stories from his yeshiva days. A teacher would point to a passage in Talmud, he told us, then he'd ask the student to identify the passage in that location four pages over. Because of the great difficulty of giving the correct answer, some students memorized entire portions of Talmud.

When I signed up for the ten-week Talmud class, I found out what my friends were talking about. During that time, we were to study a small portion of one chapter in one tractate—the subject-related sections by which Talmud is organized. Although we studied in English, rabbis master portions of Talmud in Aramaic and Hebrew, the language in which the Talmud is written.

For our class, we purchased two books—a reference guide and a student's edition of the chapter we were going to study, with the English on the page next to the Hebrew-Aramaic. Before we began our study, Rabbi Stein pointed out each of the Hebrew symbols, including those that indicated where Mishnah stopped and Gemara began.

For ten weeks, we studied a portion of Jewish law that concerned itself with what to do if you found an object that someone had apparently lost, spun off from Deuteronomy 22:1–3. After reading the passage, Rabbi Stein asked what questions it left unanswered. One importance of Talmud, he said, was that it teaches us to ask questions. If you come up with a question that the rabbis had already thought of, it's supposed to be a sign of the most outstanding level of brilliance. "Coming up with an original idea is wonderful," says Rabbi Stein, "but anticipating the arguments of the rabbis is a sign that you may be as brilliant as they were!"

Contrary to what I'd been taught in school, there *are* stupid questions within Jewish debate. One story that Rabbi Stein told us involved the most famous question in Gemara. The problem it was addressing was this: say you had a house with an open field and a bird falls inside your property. Is it yours? Rabbi Yirmiyah asked, "What if it falls halfway in and halfway out?"

For that, he supposedly got kicked out of yeshiva. The question was too ridiculous to be answered.

I found this intriguing. A superficial reading of Talmud could easily have led me to believe that lots of supposedly silly questions were tossed around by the rabbis. But this wasn't true. The extensiveness of the questioning had to do with making sure no stone remained unturned in their quest to find standards of justice. If a question fell outside what seemed a reasonable topic for debate, it was thrown out—sometimes, apparently, along with the rabbi. Their goal, I began to see, was to find reasonable standards of justice, and surely this was worth whatever amount of haggling was necessary.

Once, Rabbi G. told our small group that he had asked a "stupid" question in yeshiva. His rabbi, who was much shorter than Rabbi G., commanded him to pull a chair over. Rabbi G. obeyed. "The rabbi then climbed onto the chair and gave me a slap in the face," Rabbi G. laughed. "I was careful after that."

At any rate, when Rabbi Stein asked us what questions this passage in Deuteronomy, concerning ownership of a lost object, generated, he was bombarded with responses: "Should you pick up an object you find or should you leave it where it is? Should you advertise that you found it? If you *do* take it, how long before it can be considered yours? If it's a donkey you find, and the owner returns, should he reimburse you for its upkeep? What if the donkey has babies while it's in your possession? How do you know if someone left it there on purpose? If you take it home, can you use it? Can you use what it produces? Does it matter if the object belongs to a Jew or Gentile?" On and on they went. I had never spent so much time on questions during a study, and I suddenly realized how much more deeply it allows you to plunge into a subject.

One Talmudic rabbi asserted that if there were no distinguishing marks on the item, such as a common coin, that might identify the owner, the finder could pick it up and claim it. Such comments spawned dozens of additional problems and questions, and Talmud veers off in mind-boggling directions before returning to the question at hand. Sometimes you even have to figure out what the question is from the discussion.

For our subject, another Talmudic rabbi quoted Mishnah as claiming that if the lost item consists of scattered produce, the finder can keep it. But how do you determine that? asked another. And how scattered is scattered? Is it in a pile? Does it look like it's been blown off a pack animal? Is it lying in such a way that it looks like it's been placed there unintentionally? The question they're looking for, explains Rabbi Stein, is this: "Is someone coming back for this lost item?"

After much haggling and quoting from myriad texts, one Talmudic rabbi suggests a measurement that would seem to help determine whether someone would be returning for the lost item. If it's more than a *kav* of grain, he says, it's valuable and the loser will return to claim it. Rabbi Stein directs us to a book that explains the measurement. Then we go back to Talmud, where another scholar disagrees with the first rabbi's reasoning. "The model doesn't work," he says. Although the value of this amount of grain is high, the effort to regain it might be high, also.

Rabbi Stein goes to the chalkboard and writes the problem in diagram form; numerous combinations could change the outcome. A high value of grain and a low level of effort needed to reclaim it is an indication that the owner would probably return for it. One must leave the item where it is. A low value of grain and high level of effort indicates the owner probably won't return; one can take the lost item.

But a high value of grain with a high level of effort needed to regain it, well, the owner might come back because of the high value, or he might leave it because of the high effort it would take to find it. In this case, the scholars finally agreed, *teyku*—let it stand unresolved. There is no answer.

But then the rabbis are off to debate dozens of other considerations: What if the object is lost during a natural disaster?

Perhaps the object seems invaluable but is, in reality, extremely valuable to the owner—does it change the value of an item if the loser is rich instead of poor?

Although my head was spinning, I was increasingly seeing these long debates in a new light. Although the rabbis certainly loved to study and debate, they also had a consuming desire to live justly, to be fair to everyone in all the affairs of everyday life. "Jewish tradition," explained Rabbi Stein, "begins in ensuring absolute justice."

Even though only a tiny percentage of American Jews look to Talmudic law—*halakhah*—for their daily decisions, its principle is firmly entrenched. Out of Talmud, for instance, has come the Jewish appreciation for *tzeddakah*, or charity. One must never cheat or steal, and one must always be considerate of those less fortunate. Even those who are poor are obligated to give, says Talmud.

An "eye for an eye" (a passage Christians often misinterpret) is explained in Talmud as a passage ensuring that no one will take vengeance over another, killing someone, for instance, to avenge a lost eye. As for the death penalty, Talmud explains that there must be two witnesses to a crime, neither of whom is related to the other or to the accused. The witnesses have to warn the criminal in advance that what he's about to do could result in the death penalty, and the criminal has to acknowledge the warning and commit the crime anyway while the witnesses are watching. This rendered it almost impossible to receive the death penalty. In addition, if the court put more than one person to death in a period of seventy years, it was shamed by all as a bloody court.

The purpose of Talmud, I was finally beginning to understand, wasn't to put endless nooses of law around the Jewish neck but to protect the defenseless, to ensure that people were treated with respect, and to provide *halakhah*, or rules, to guide Jews in their business and personal interactions with others.

Most interesting of all, of the two most famous rabbinical schools of thought, Hillel and Shammai, Talmudic scholars sided with Hillel in all but about six of their debates. Shammai, the strict and often harsh rabbinical leader, lost to the lenient and kind Hillel. Interesting but not surprising. For the Jewish love of study, at its heart, is about relationship with humankind and with God. Not only am I utterly taken by the depth with which they approach these great loves, I believe everyone would benefit from such attention to detail when it concerns the way they treat other people.

Although the Jewish love of study is reflected in the lengthy arguments of Talmud, it's also evident in the passion with which Jews regard Torah. I remember one evening at the Colorado retreat, when one of the men prepared to carry Torah down the aisles for people to touch and kiss. As he reached the edge of the *mechitza,* however, Rivka, who seemed to be the matriarch of the group, suddenly sprang over to him and took the Torah scroll from his hands. The man looked startled and unsure what to do, but he handed the scroll to her.

Gently, Rivka gave the scroll to a young woman who stood stunned for a few moments. Then, cradling the scroll in her arms, she began to weep as she carried it down the women's aisle. Soon all the women were crying. Reluctantly, the young woman reached the end of the aisle and handed the scroll to the men who were waiting for it. As she sat down, several women went over to her, all of them hugging and weeping with utter abandonment.

Rivka sat down by me and explained that she had taken the Torah because when the men walked down the women's aisle and the women bent to kiss Torah, they sometimes missed and kissed the man. "That's improper," she informed me. "Men and women are not supposed even to touch, and here the women are accidentally kissing them!" I grinned, wondering if this was the real reason she had taken Torah from the men.

I remembered one evening at Temple Emanu-El, when I had held Torah and experienced similar feelings as these women. It was during a holiday service, and Rabbi Kaiserman had asked me if I'd hold Torah while the Ten Commandments were read. Although I had held it in the past and even danced with it in other settings, it always rattled me to be asked. The rabbi, noticing the surprised expression on my face, said, "It's OK. You just have to *hold* it, not *read* it." Everyone laughed.

I stood on one side of the Torah, holding the wooden handle, while a man about my height stood on the other side. Slowly we walked backwards, unrolling the scroll. An aura of excitement and awe filled the room. It didn't matter that most of these people had watched Torah being unscrolled hundreds of times or that few in this room of liberal Jews believed God had literally dictated Torah to Moses. They loved Torah! They kissed Torah!

The large scroll stood open before the congregation, held high for everyone to see. Then Rabbi Debra Robbins began sliding a tiny silver pointer along the Hebrew text, reading the Ten Commandments first in Hebrew, then in English. I stood before a people whose devotion to God had endured for thousands of years, despite seeming abandonment, severe punishment, and catastrophic change. Tears welled up in my eyes, for I too loved this sacred text. I felt a sense of awe being around the Jews—the people who had brought this scripture into the world—and I was thrilled by the mere sight of the beautiful Torah scroll—a replica of the scrolls that had been in existence for hundreds of years.

It's difficult to overestimate the Jewish love of Torah. In his book *Mandarins, Jews, and Missionaries,* author Michael Pollak tells of the horrible siege in 1642 on the city of Kaifeng by Chinese forces, in which they destroyed a section of the dikes lining the Yellow River and flooded the city, killing as many as three hundred thousand people and virtually destroying the city.

Jewish survivors, who had lost their synagogue, searched the devastated city for pieces of their sacred books, which had all been swept away by the flood. "The recovered Torahs," writes Pollak, "though severely damaged, were pieced together, producing one usable Torah and several other portions of scripture."[3]

I remember one evening at a Jewish service when I was gently corrected by a friend for laying my Bible on the floor. Jews don't treat their holy book in this manner, I was told. If someone drops a *sefer* Torah (a Torah scroll made from kosher materials and penned by a scribe) during a service, the entire congregation is supposed to fast for forty days. Once, I saw a young child accidentally drop her prayer book in an Orthodox synagogue. Her sister gently picked it up, kissed it, and placed it back on a chair.

One of the most beautiful ceremonies I ever attended was the completion of a *sefer* Torah by a professional scribe. A family, members of the synagogue receiving the scroll, had offered their backyard for the service and, when I arrived on the lovely spring Sabbath morning, several people were piling tables high with plates of fruit, fresh vegetables, and desserts. A canopy sheltered the table on which the Torah would be placed later in the day.

A CD with lively Jewish music was cranked up as people talked and ate. Soon, however, the back door of the house was flung open and several men danced ceremonially outdoors with the

Torah. The crowd erupted with singing and clapping and weeping. The Torah scroll was placed under the canopy, and the rabbi-scribe took his seat in front of it.

A Torah scroll usually takes a couple of years to complete. The first year is spent making the parchment alone, which is stitched with kosher animal gut. Indeed, the entire Torah must be constructed with prescribed materials, including the ink and even the pen with which it's written.

After the scroll is prepared, a professional scribe, known as a *sofer setam,* begins writing it by hand, which takes another year. It's painstakingly written letter by letter, with no punctuation and no vowels. The three columns are so perfectly written that they appear to have been computer-justified. A *sefer* Torah may cost as much as $100,000.

Because the earliest known Torah scrolls contain occasional gaps between sentences, current scribes continue to copy Torah with precisely the same spaces. Although no one knows exactly why this occurred, there are a number of drashes, or stories. One story is that these are the places where the ancient scribes paused to go and ask questions.

As the scribe nears the end of Torah, he leaves the final eighteen letters unwritten. (In Jewish mysticism, the number 18 symbolizes life.) During the service I attended, these final letters were auctioned to members who, one by one, placed their hands on the hand of the scribe as he completed each letter.

It's a great mitzvah to "write" a letter of Torah, and a few people donated large sums of money for theirs. If the donor was female, someone would place a white cloth on the arm of the rabbi so she could "write" her letter, as it isn't permitted in Orthodox circles for men and women to touch. At the end of the ceremony, all members who had been unable to donate money were called to the canopy to place their hands on the rabbi's arm as he wrote the final letter. Several sobbed loudly with joy.

The writing of eighteen letters took an hour and a half, and when the last letter had been written, the men grabbed the four poles of the canopy, along with the Torah, and we began the procession through the streets of Dallas on our way to the synagogue.

The men and women gave themselves over to uninhibited singing and dancing. Cars pulled over so their occupants could watch. People were drawn from their homes, perching on their front porches and curbs as we danced by. Occasionally, the men holding the Torah would become ecstatic, having to stop their progress so they could abandon themselves to dancing.

I was utterly drawn in by the joy. I couldn't help but remember David, who leapt and danced with all his strength as a group of men carried the ark to the house of Obed-edom the Gittite (2 Samuel 6:12–16). As always, I felt transported back in time, caught up in a joyous ritual that, in some form, had existed for many hundreds of years. The physical beauty of this Torah and the wisdom and history that it contained seemed to me worth dancing about.

One woman, who looked to be in her eighties, had been dancing almost since I arrived with a bottle of wine balanced on her head. On the way to synagogue, as someone pushed her in a wheelchair, she continued with a Coke can (no one wanted to risk a broken wine bottle in the middle of the street) and wiggled her upper body in her dance of joy.

Arriving at the synagogue, everyone danced in the parking lot for about fifteen minutes. They then moved to the foyer and danced for fifteen more. Finally, the procession moved into the sanctuary, where the women were forced to stand in a small space in the back of the room behind the *mechitza* while the men continued to dance with abandon near the ark. That didn't faze the old woman one bit. She discarded her Coke can, grabbed a bottle of wine that someone had brought along, and resumed her dance.

It was in a more liberal setting that I was allowed to hold and dance with Torah, and it was an experience I'll always treasure.

A local *havurah* had folded when their rabbi had been offered a position in a synagogue outside the Dallas area, and the group had donated everything, including a *sefer* Torah, to Ruach Torah, the group with whom I regularly worshiped and studied. Joseph, the *gabbai,* decided to surprise Hesha with its presentation.

The following Sabbath evening, about forty of us sat in Joseph's living room, preparing to begin the evening of worship. After a couple of songs, Hesha led us to symbolically cast our cares into a trash heap in the center of the circle. "Just remember," she said, "that a pile of doo-doo makes good fertilizer from which to bring good things." It was typical Hesha.

As we stood and closed our eyes, supposedly preparing for another meditation, two women, Elayne and Happy, slipped out to get the Torah. Hesha opened her eyes, which glistened with tears as Joseph handed her the scroll. As the scroll was passed from hand to hand, Hesha pointed out the brass emblem dangling from its cover and the stunning embroidery, asking us to carefully examine its beauty.

Suddenly, someone slipped a CD in and the dancing began. The person holding the Torah moved to the center of the circle, dancing, as everyone gathered in closely, clapping to the rhythm of the music. My *chevruta* handed me the beautiful scroll and pulled me to the center of the room. Of course, I wasn't holding it correctly, and Hesha came over to gently show me how. Then, after a few minutes, she called for me, still holding the Torah, to lead everyone in a "snake" dance throughout the house.

Eventually, Hesha retrieved the Torah and placed it carefully on the table. She was hesitant to unroll it because we weren't in a synagogue, but someone said that Torah sanctifies whatever place it's in, so Hesha began to unfold it as we gathered around.

I had never looked at a Torah so closely, and I was mesmerized. It was obvious that a great deal of love and careful attention had been given to create it. The script was perfect and beautiful. I remembered reading that the first Torah was said to have been written in black fire on white fire. The atmosphere in the room as we stood around the scroll reproduced a bit of this intensity.

After talking a bit, Hesha's son held the Torah in front of the room while we recited the blessing for returning Torah to the ark. Then the cover was replaced, and it was gently laid on a table in the library, where it would rest until an ark could be built. Before Hesha left that evening, she stopped by the room, bent over, and kissed the Torah. It was for her the greatest gift the *havurah* could have received.

The Hebrew Bible is basically the same as the Protestant Old Testament, although it's arranged a bit differently. Tanakh, as the Hebrew Bible is called, is an acronym for Torah, Neviim, and Kesuvim: the law, the prophets, and the writings, in that order. The law is, of course, Torah, or the first five books of the Bible; Neviim stands for the prophets and Kesuvim for the writings.

Still, even with its apparent likenesses, I never get the same feeling reading Tanakh as I do reading the Christian Old Testament. The translations aren't drastically different, but the "atmosphere" of Tanakh is distinctively Jewish. Various names of God are left intact, for instance, such as Abram's cry to *"HASHEM/ELOHIM"* (Genesis 15:8) and God's declaration to Abram that he is *"El Shaddai"* (Genesis 17:1).

I've begun to understand the importance of this. For instance, when one wants strength, praying to *El Shaddai*—God Almighty—conjures up feelings of God's attribute of power. Because YHVH isn't supposed to be pronounced, meditating on the form and shape of these letters can instill a sense of mystery. I've found that these seemingly minor changes give reading scripture a new feel, a sense of freshness.

Other words are left intact that are distinctly recognizable or meaningful to the Jewish reader: matzos rather than our translation of "unleavened bread" (Genesis 19:3), *shofar* instead of our "trumpet" (Genesis 19:19), *Kohanim* in place of "priest" (Leviticus 21:1), and tzitzit instead of "fringe" (Numbers 15:37), to name a few.

Holidays are identified, such as the festival of Succos (Sukkot) and, when enumerating clean and unclean animals, Tanakh takes greater care with their identity, as this is important to keeping kosher. All of this has made reading Tanakh more Jewishly flavorful and given me a better understanding of scripture (Deuteronomy 9:11 and elsewhere and Leviticus 23:33).

Yet that isn't why studying with the Jews is so delicious. When I first began studying with Hesha's group, for instance, I learned that mystical Jews approach scripture on four levels. *Peshat,* the first level, is the surface meaning of the verse. *Remez* delves into interpretation, which is a level that Jews plunge into and play with. *Derash* is allegory, which is another level that can go in numerous directions, and *sod* is the secret or mystical meaning, which is found by those who know how to interpret it in kabbalistic texts.

Studying with the Jews transformed the Bible for me. For years, I believed that the importance of scripture lay merely in its literal interpretation. Although I believed the Bible had meaning for everyday life, I sought to find it by simple interpretations that stayed close to a literal meaning. For instance, I might take a verse in the Hebrew Bible about God supposedly commanding the Israelites to "completely destroy" the people of another land and apply that, say, as our need to "completely destroy" sin in our lives. But that was as far as I'd take it.

For most of my adult years, I'd set aside what we called a "quiet time" each day, in which I'd devotionally read the Bible for fifteen to thirty minutes, looking for some kind of personal application. Later, I was taught that the way to study the Bible is to take it apart, word for word, following formulas and procedures. The idea was to look at the original languages, the culture, the context.

That was all well and good, but the goal, which wasn't so well and good, was merely to find the passage's most probable, literal meaning and then to attach a personal, modern application. Eventually, the inconsistencies of this kind of study caused me to reject this method.

Although it wasn't the Jews but a new church and pastor, George Mason, who ushered me into a new understanding of the Bible, it was the Jews who began to turn the world of my Bible upside down and inside out.

The Jews, as I've said, can discuss a scripture passage for hours, and the interpretations and spiritual meanings they come up with unimaginably enrich the Bible. Through my studies with Rabbi G. and with Hesha, I also became enamored with the mystical aspects of scripture. This kind of study was worlds away from the simple quiet time that I was used to.

How grateful I was that I could re-imagine everything in scripture as deeply symbolic, with hidden meanings that could be revealed layer by layer and mysteries that plunged me into a world of spiritual adventure and intrigue.

I had missed out on so much of the real richness and depth of the Bible by becoming stuck in the world of *Peshat*. The real magic, I began to see, isn't in a literal reading but in a metaphorical one.

The garden, for instance, has always been used in a symbolic manner by storytellers. In Jewish mystical thought, the garden is one of seven worlds where pure souls dwell until they enter an earthly body and where all but the evil will return to await the coming of the *Moshiach,* or Messiah. God once left this "place," and the Song of Songs, in kabbalistic thought, is about his return.

The questions that a metaphorical reading of this passage raises are endless, and they are precisely what makes this story so enchanting. Because "the garden" is a metaphor for great loveliness and perfection, I automatically wonder why humankind is prone to leave these places, as "Adam and Eve" did. I ponder the meaning of nakedness, of our vulnerability before God and one another. I muse about the godlikeness of our knowledge and morality.

The story of the garden portrays a writer's wrestling, through the mode of story, with the beginning of evil. When I read this story metaphorically, I wonder, Is there an actual evil force that opposes God? Are they equal? How does it entice us? How do we affect one another? What have been the results of our waywardness?

The image of the garden evokes many more questions and interpretations, and when I read the Bible this way—looking for questions instead of answers, playing with the metaphors and stories and language and symbolism—it leaps into a realm of genuine wonder and intrigue.

I began to understand this metaphorical way of reading scripture better when I compared it to the way we interpret dreams. For many years, I didn't understand the rich, personal symbolism of dreams. I'd get up in the morning, remember my dreams briefly, then go on with my day, disregarding or forgetting them entirely.

As I began to read about dream interpretation, however, that changed dramatically. Many modern dream analysts believe that our best interpretations are personal ones: What do those symbols mean to *you,* and what is the dream, in the context of your life right now, saying? Often, if you write out your dream, the words you use will relate dramatic meaning that otherwise wouldn't be apparent.

Not long ago, for instance, I had a brief dream about a friend. We were standing in a room alone when suddenly something fell from his mouth. It was a prosthetic tongue! How strange, I thought in my dream. Then he began talking, and I was astonished to hear how plainly he spoke. How can a person speak without a tongue, I wondered?

As I lay in bed thinking about this dream's symbolism, I quickly recognized that the dream was telling me that the deepest communication, often the clearest, is accomplished without words. My friend not only didn't have a tongue, which symbolized language, he actually spoke most clearly when his prosthetic one had fallen from his mouth—when he *really* had no tongue and thus no literal way of speaking.

Because I was going through some intense spiritual and personal changes in my life at the time of this dream and had had other, similar dreams, I knew that the message to me was that I should look for guidance in ways other than through verbal teachings and that I should listen to other cues, picking up on other signals that would help me find direction. Metaphor, story, and symbolism are far more meaningful than any literal event.

In the same way, one of the greatest gifts that the Jews have given me has been this ability to see scripture with the same metaphorical and symbolic sense of wonder. I've replaced my need to find answers, often simplistic ones, with a passion to formulate questions. Instead of a bland literalism, I now dig for the mysterious and hidden meanings in the Bible, playing with a story's many spiritual implications.

That new approach, with its uniquely Jewish love of spiritual adventure and exploration, has, most important, allowed me to embrace a much broader and more magnificent vision of God. What a gift I've been given, and how deeply I've come to love those who have given it.

CHAPTER FOUR

Discovering the Passionate Hebrew God

During a recent service at Chabad, with the service in full swing, Rabbi G.'s two young children began to busily explore the entire synagogue. Up and down the aisles they went, quietly, stopping now and then to look carefully at a congregant. After they tired of this, they headed toward the front of the room, flipping aside the cloth that covered the table where Rabbi G. stood chanting Torah; then they crawled underneath, where they could hide. Occasionally, the children simply stood beside their father, clinging to his leg or leaning against him.

Because they were quiet, they didn't disrupt the service and the people prayed undisturbed. A while later, Rabbi G. completed the prayers and moved to the edge of the *mechitza* where he could best address both the men and women. As he spoke, his youngest child crept through his legs and hid behind the curtain of the ark, which stood directly behind him. She probably would have gone unnoticed except that she began waving through the curtain.

"Leah, this isn't a performance," Rabbi G. whispered gently. "It's a prayer service." As she scrambled away from the curtain, a friend of the rabbi's guided her back to an area where she could play. I couldn't help but wonder at the freedom children had in certain synagogues and the tenderness with which they were treated.

This was hardly the first time I'd seen this kind of interplay between a rabbi and his children. Once, during the chanting of a prayer, a very young child squirmed from her mother and scampered to the front of the synagogue where her father stood. The rabbi, without pausing from his chanting, picked her up and continued to hold her as he prayed.

Still another Hasidic rabbi was pictured, a few years ago, on the front page of the religion section of the *Dallas Morning News*. The picture was taken as he sat teaching a Sunday morning class, his three children gathered around him, one sitting on his lap, one standing as close as she could get, and a third with his head on the rabbi's shoulder.

As I was recently telling my husband these stories, he said, "Isn't that a great picture of the Jews' relationship with God?" Yes, I thought, just as the children clamored for their father's attention, the Jews can't get close enough to God. Just as Rabbi G. exuded patience with his children's antics, so the Jews see God's infinite patience with humankind. Just as the children were welcomed by their father as he chanted prayers, so the Jews believe all are welcome who run to God.

As I was growing up, this picture of God as Father was one I was most familiar with. Indeed, "father" was the metaphor I most frequently associated with God. In Judaism, though I've rarely heard this metaphor used, I see it *portrayed* all the time. The Jews' intimacy with God is always evident; their family ties with God shine through in every prayer service and study.

What has been most fascinating to me about the Jewish view of God, however, is that although they embrace this familial aspect of God, they see it as one attribute existing alongside others. God is a Being of love to the Jews, yes, but God is also, equally, fire and mystery. For a Jew, this complex Being isn't only accepted; he is adored.

I remember a book I saw in a bookstore many years ago titled *Your God Is Too Small.* That sums up well what God was, in the past, to me. Studying and worshiping with the Jews has helped change that.

One aspect of the Jewish view of God is that he is a Being of infinite love. On my shelf, I have two books sitting side by side. Both are by Abraham Joshua Heschel—the much-loved Jewish writer, professor, and scholar who died in 1972. A mere look at these two books reveals a lot about the Jewish view of God as a Being of love. One of these books is *Man's Quest for God,* first published in 1954. It's a small book, 151 pages long. The second, written the following year, is titled *God in Search of Man.* Its length? 426 pages. Very telling. God's pursuit of humankind is much greater than is humankind's quest for God.

In the foreword to *God in Search of Man,* the author's daughter, Susannah Heschel, points out that this theme is a "central concern" of her father's writings. Rejecting Aristotle's reference to the One as the "Unmoved Mover," Heschel describes God as the "Most Moved Mover." God is in need of human beings, Heschel writes. What is the pathos of God but that God is deeply affected by what humans do?[1]

"You know always in your heart that you need God more than everything," writes the famous Jewish philosopher Martin Buber, "but do you not know too that God needs you—in the fulness of His eternity needs you? How would man exist, how would you exist, if God did not need him, did not need you?"[2]

As usual, the Hasidim depict God's need in a humorous and straightforward manner. Wiesel tells the story of the Rebbe of Berditchev—Rabbi Levi-Yitzhak Derbaremdiger—who was known to demand answers of God and, when he didn't get them, would draw his own conclusions. Once, writes Wiesel, the rebbe "offered God a bargain: 'We shall give You our sins and, in return, You will grant us Your pardon. By the way, You come out ahead. Without our sins, what would You do with Your pardon?'"[3]

Another rabbi used the example of two young lovers whom he was counseling to illustrate God's relationship with us. "As passionate as you two children are about each other," he said, "as great a need as you have of this one you love, that is the way God felt when he made the world."[4] There is that phrase again: God needs us. His joy over us compares with the joy of two star-struck lovers, needed by each other, loved to distraction.

The Hasidic branch of Judaism takes the word *need* very seriously. God doesn't need us merely in an emotional manner. We actually strengthen God. Doing mitzvot (obeying God's commands) and *chesed* (doing acts of kindness) "produce all manner of spiritual delight and pleasure for Hashem," writes one Hasidic teacher. Such delight and pleasure "greatly empower Hashem."[5]

Although I've always loved the passionate and intense God depicted in the Hebrew scriptures, I didn't realize, until the past several years, that the Jews so deeply emphasize love in their religion. This shortsightedness of mine seems utterly strange to me now because it's the Hebrew scriptures that describe a God who, in an almost desperate manner, longs to be close to humankind.

Although the mountains may be moved and the hills may falter, says God through the prophet Isaiah, my love will never die (Isaiah 54:10). The God of the Hebrews never gives up on his beloved. God will do anything to win a heart, to draw it intimately close, to reclaim a waning relationship. The prophets spoke of a God who longed for his people, who tirelessly pursued them, who loved to distraction.

As I've worshiped with the Jews, I've seen them engage this God of love firsthand. One evening, during my weekly study with Rabbi G., he pointed out that the Bible says God is the God of Abraham, the God of Jacob, and the God of Isaac, making each phrase distinctive from the others.

"Why?" he asked, in the traditional lilting question that Jews ask after a puzzling passage: "Why doesn't it just say the God of Abraham, Jacob, and Isaac?"

The answer is that God is the God of each individual. God will be what Abraham needs, what Jacob needs, and what Isaac needs. God will be what you need and what I need. God loves us this much. Although the Jews believe that God deals with them as a people and not just individually, I've also come to understand that they see God in a very personal way, as having a personal relationship with each human being.

"God loves, loves, loves us," Hesha would often say in her always-excited manner when talking about God. "God's heart bursts with love." Always I felt as if Hesha had just returned from an ecstatic union with the God of love and I was privileged to soak up the rays that continued to linger. Hesha's intimate descriptions of God transformed me and others emotionally into the Bride of Solomon's Song, and I sometimes thought I could actually hear God's heart beating for us.

The God of the Hebrews is God the romantic pursuer—an enchanted lover who showers gifts on his beloved. Isaiah portrays God beautifully in this way, writing that Israel would be encased with jewels. Her "floors" would be made of gems and her foundation with sapphires. The windows through which Israel gazed upon the world would be framed of rubies and her gates of carbuncle stones. Indeed, says Isaiah, Israel's entire boundary would be inlaid with precious stones (Isaiah 54:11–12).

The story I see in the Hebrew Bible is about the greatest love affair humankind has ever known. No star-struck couple compares. If I had to summarize the story in a sentence, it would be that God will do anything, go anywhere, and stop at nothing in order to win the hearts of those he loves. The Jewish God of fire is wholly and completely passionate, and a consuming desire drives him to relentlessly look for and pursue his beloved.

The word translated "elect" in the Greek Testament, which has been used by some Christians as an indication that God chooses, or predestines, only an "elect" number for salvation, can also be translated "to take" or "to win." In classical Greek, the word was used to refer to the seizure of a city.[6] Both phrases—"to take" and "to win"—have romantic implications.

I remember a discussion years ago at a writers' conference in which a man expressed his dislike of the term *taken* from an erotic poem we were reading in our small study group. The women—attorneys, conference leaders, senior pastors, psychologists, writers, and other professionals—unanimously disagreed. The thought of "being taken" (please don't misconstrue this as any form of rape or unwanted, forceful sexual contact) is a romantic phrase and one we all liked.

God seeks to win and to take us. His pursuit is active. A passage in the Greek Testament talks about Satan's incessant roaming, seeking to devour. I like to twist this to reflect God. God wanders about, longing for humankind, devouring us with love. In all my many images of God from numerous religions, this Hebraic depiction is one that touches me most deeply.

Love, however, is meant to be shared, and the Jews I know seek to return God's adoration, arousing their hearts through study and worship and meditation. It isn't enough to use rituals, powerful as they are, to draw close to God. They want to infuse those rituals with fervent and passionate hearts.

In the *Shema,* Rabbi G. tells me, the word translated as "heart" here isn't *lev* but *levav*. The doubling of the middle letter suggests a plural form, he explains, and is thus interpreted by the Talmud to mean that a man is commanded to love God with the whole of his dual heart, both "animalistic" and "godly." Nothing in us is to remain unsinged. We are to be consumed with love for God.

This is exactly what I see in many Jews with whom I worship and study, and I'm astonished that I ever thought of their religion as legalistic. How skewed my view of Judaism was. The Jews exude a warmth and passion for God that I feel as soon as I'm in their presence. And their enthusiasm and spirituality is contagious.

One year, I had planned to attend a Jewish holiday service, got confused about the date, and showed up after the service ended. Everyone had left the synagogue except for one young man who was quietly and unhurriedly cleaning up. "I was just going outside to look at the stars," he said. "Come join me."

We walked outside and stood for a few moments in silence. I felt the same sense of inexplicable peace I had felt during the Sabbath in Colorado and at other times when I've been with the Jews during their sacred days. "Look," the young man said, pointing toward the sky. "Rosh Hashanah is officially over. There are three stars."

Although seeing three stars in close proximity to one another is simply a method that was used before clocks were invented, it's a lovely tradition that Jews have held onto. As we stood looking at the sky that evening, neither of us felt the need to talk. I felt a sense of sacred presence and, looking at the young man, I noticed a look of intense joy spread across his face. He seemed (how else to put it?) infatuated with God.

Although my dictionary doesn't give many positive definitions for *infatuation,* it does give one. Infatuation is, it says, an "extravagant love or desire." It is marked by a "strong attachment and unreasoning love."

What a beautiful description! The Jews' longtime relationship with God has been full of what seems like abandonment and betrayal and neglect. They have been exiled and massacred in more than one holocaust and have been the recipients of more hatred than probably any other people in history. Although the faith of some has been shaken, and some have wondered how God could allow these kinds of horrors, the Jews I've come to know emerge from these questions and challenges with a love that, in the face of their history, can only be seen as extravagant and unreasoning.

There's a beautiful story from an ancient Jewish text that gives a mystical interpretation of the cherubim that sat on top of the ark of the covenant. The tale derives from supposedly conflicting texts in Chronicles and Exodus. One of these states that the cherubim were turned away from one another; the other claims they faced each other. Why? we might ask in typical Jewish fashion.

The text explains that because the cherubim represented the relationship of love between God and his people, when these angels were turned from each other, this meant that Israel had turned from God (it seems more accurate to me that only one turned away: Israel. God never turned away). But when Israel lived in devotion to God, the cherubim not only faced each other, they were "intertwined in the embrace of love."

Says the text: "When the Israelites came up on the Pilgrim Festivals the curtain would be removed for them and the cherubim shown to them, their bodies interlocked with one another, and they would say to them, 'Look, you are beloved before God as the love between man and woman.'"[7]

Growing up, I never fully understood that it was the Jews who first gave the world this personal, passionate God of love. How strange, I now think. Although I believe one God is over all and loves all people of all religions equally, I don't think I would have ever experienced the fullness of divine love without the Hebrew Testament. Such a testament is only "old," as many Christians refer to it, in its age and history. It will, however, always be "new" to me, for the love and the God it reveals are timeless.

Alongside this God of love in Judaism, though, lies the supposedly paradoxical God of fire. Although I've caught glimpses of this God all my life, it wasn't until I was in my thirties, when I began my love affair with Judaism, that I found myself fully immersed in the singular God of both passionate love and volcanic eruptions. This God burned a bush without consuming it, set a mountain on fire, erupted in passionate anger, supposedly struck people dead who came too close, and blinded people with his mere angelic representation.

One evening, at a Ruach Torah service, Hesha was discussing the story of the sons of Aaron who, scripture indicates, were struck down by God's fire for offering a sacrifice that God had not commanded them to offer (Leviticus 10:1). As Hesha spoke, she pointed out that the men didn't realize what kind of power they were dealing with, that coming directly into God's presence is like standing in water while coming in contact with a massive volt of electricity. It wasn't a willful act of God to kill anyone, she said, but a result of being in a place where you shouldn't be.

As I thought about this, I came to realize that seeing God as a Being of fire is very different from seeing God as a Being that *willfully causes* harm and destruction. If God is an omnipotent Being that infuses and gives life to everything in the universe, I thought, it makes sense that he is also a Being that we can never *fully* be in the presence of without risking getting burned.

Rabbi Niles Elliot Goldstein tells of an encounter he once had with a grizzly while he was hiking alone in a remote area of Denali National Park in Alaska. Remembering the bear's approach, Rabbi Goldstein later struggled to write of the feelings that had surged through him at the time. The sensation was raw and primal, he wrote, and he felt a "naked, unbridled fear" accompanied by a "strange sort of reverence."

Rabbi Goldstein compares this experience to an encounter with God. "In classical Jewish thought," he writes, "it is only after one has experienced the fear of God that life gains complete clarity, that a person fully and finally understands his or her place in the cosmic whole. Standing there, scared, vulnerable, and alone in the presence of a being far more powerful and attuned to nature than I could ever hope to be, gave me a hint of what it must be like to behold the Divine Presence, to experience a brief, mystical, life-altering flash of transcendence."

Rabbi Goldstein adds that an inscription written above the Holy Ark in many synagogues around the world says it best: *"Da lifney mi atah omed:* Know before Whom you stand."[8]

Although I hold a degree in anthropology and have studied the religions of many cultures around the world, the Jews' view of the majesty and mystery of God is uniquely intriguing to me.

Undoubtedly, that's because Judaism is so intricately intertwined with my own religion (Christianity), which mostly rejects or ignores this fearsome aspect of God—an aspect I've always been personally attracted to.

The Jews do not see any contradiction in a God being one of love and one of fire. They simply embrace and adore a Being who encompasses both facets. In fact, they get *really excited* about this kind of God. Jews cover their eyes as they recite the *Shema,* and they whisper the *Amidah*—another prayer in Jewish liturgy— because they are coming closer to God. Indeed, one explanation of the order of prayer in a Jewish service is that it represents an ascent through various mystical worlds, rising higher and higher until one encounters God. The approach, although confident and secure, is filled with awe.

This became clear to me one evening as I sat reading the scripture that describes Moses, his face shining, descending from Mount Sinai. When the people saw him, they were terrified and withdrew. Their fear caused them to run from God. Moses, however, felt an excitement that caused him to ask God for more.

The Jews I've come to know are, like Moses, aware of and drawn to God's majesty. Their eyes light up with wonder when they speak of him. God is a magnificent Being whom they adore— a king whom they respectfully approach, even with the knowledge that he is passionately in love with them.

A Christian friend of mine, whom I'll call Richard, once told me an interesting story related to this view of God. Richard, a deacon in a conservative Baptist church, used to occasionally attend other churches so he could have new experiences of God. One night, he told me, he had left a worship service and was driving home when he felt an awareness of God's presence that he'd never before felt. It was so powerful, in fact, that he had to pull over to the side of the road.

There, for what seemed like hours, Richard said he was so immersed in love and in a direct experience of God that he was literally paralyzed. Unable to drive, to speak, even to move, Richard wept uncontrollably. "When I found my voice," he said, "I had to cry out to God to stop. I honestly believe if he hadn't, I would've died."

Richard confided that he had only shared this story with one other person. Not only was it too personal for him to freely share but he feared ridicule and misunderstanding. How could you die from an encounter with God? How could love be so overwhelming that you ask God to take it away?

Some years later, one of my Jewish friends described a similar encounter. She had been meditating and felt the presence of God in a way she'd never before felt. The experience overwhelmed and frightened her. Immediately, she pulled out of her meditative state and, in her words, "ran" from the encounter.

What is interesting to me is that my Christian friend described his experience in terms of love, whereas my Jewish friend described hers as a close encounter with holiness and power. Of course, I have no way of knowing whether these two friends had the same basic experience, but my guess is that they did and that they merely used different terms in keeping with their religious tradition. In a close brush with God, we struggle to describe with our limited vocabulary what we've felt but come up short. Love mingles with power, which merges into holiness. God's presence brings us forcefully into a world that overwhelms our senses and emotions.

Listening to my friends' stories, I know that I have only the faintest idea of what it means to come close to such majesty. "No human can see My face and live," God said to Moses (Exodus 33:20). The face represents the fullness of God and few, if any, humans can get this close. It isn't that God willfully would strike us dead. It's just that, like Richard, we can't handle the intensity of the moment.

Our post-death experiences, when we'll encounter God, surely will have this element of intensity. Indeed, as I've become more interested in mysticism, I tend to think this may characterize our "passing on" entirely. As Paul wrote, one day we'll know "face to face," that is, we will unite with God in a way that we can now only catch glimpses of.

Chabad, the organization affiliated with the Lubavitchers, writes this:

> After 70, 80, maybe 120 years, the soul ascends to a place above called Gan Eden, a place of ecstasy as great as the soul can receive without dissolving altogether. And what is that delight that is so overwhelming? No more than a trickle of light from the pleasure G-d[9] received from the struggle of this soul as it was below.

The Hasidim, with their elevation of intense feeling and emotion in worship, understand that ecstasy, which accompanies a direct encounter with God, will reach its culmination in the afterlife. Yet even there, God will have to "hold back" in order for us not to be engulfed and annihilated by God's unspeakable glory, love, and beauty, though we'll have all we'd ever want or could imagine.

As I've seen God through the eyes of the Jews, I've gained an entirely new respect for this magnificent Being. In the past, I've needed a God I could merely relate to, not one who struck me dumb. Now my encounters with God aren't merely about me, about my relationship with God, or about what I want or need; they are sometimes simply about God.

My vision has been expanded. My focus isn't so self-centered. There is more distance between God and me, but it isn't a relational distance. It's a distance of *being*—of understanding the gulf between who I am and who God is. God isn't quite so familiar to me. God is a Being who, though brimming with passionate, undying love, also fills the earth with bone-rattling, holy energy.

One evening, Rabbi G. began talking about how to approach God. At the lowest level is a fear that brings embarrassment and shame. This is the fear of a child, he said. At a higher level is a feeling of awe that you're going to see the king. Then, when you enter his chamber, you fall down. Love needs this kind of fear, he explains. Without it, the feeling of love is less intense, and you take the relationship for granted.

The Jews have helped propel me to this higher level.

In Judaism, however, there is a third aspect of God that I love, perhaps most of all. God is a Being of love and fire, but God, in the eyes of the Jews, is also a Being of great mystery.

A couple of years ago, my friend Karen Prager accepted an invitation to teach my Sunday school class for a couple of weeks. The men and women in my class, like so many Christians today, were clamoring to better understand Judaism, and the first morning she taught, Karen was bombarded with questions, so many, in fact, that she didn't even get to her lesson—which was OK with her.

As she fielded the questions, Karen tried to engage my class with the excitement and awe of mystery, but it quickly became too much for one man, who raised his hand and asked in perplexity, "But how do you tell the difference between superstition and reality?"

Karen's eyes sparkled with mischievousness and wonder. "It's hard in this day and age to open ourselves to mystery, isn't it?" she simply replied. She, like other Jews I know, delight in the mystery of God, and I knew that she didn't want to leave this realm—the realm of the mysterious—in order to debate it on an intellectual level.

Karen and other Jews with whom I've worshiped have taught me that for every aspect of God that we discover, hundreds more are hidden away, beckoning us to take a closer look. With every answer that seems to reveal itself, hundreds of additional questions unfold.

God is a Being of enchanting mystery. We can try to describe God, but words will ultimately fall short. God pulsates with splendor, permeates the universe, strikes our hearts with love and terror, penetrates us with his unfathomable wisdom and knowledge—but what God *is,* we can never know, at least on an intellectual basis. Writes Rabbi Milton Steinberg, "God will forever elude us; and where He does not elude, [God will] overwhelm us."[10]

Man's ignorance of God, writes Steinberg, is, in Judaism, pronounced everywhere. God reminded Moses that humankind can't see his face (Exodus 33:20). David cried that knowledge of God was beyond him, exalted; he was "incapable of it" (Psalm 139:6.) "God thunders marvelously . . . [and] does wonders that we do not comprehend," says Job (37:5). Such respect for the mystery of God permeates Hebrew thought.

Being with the Jews casts me into a sea of delight with this kind of mystery. It magnifies my experience of God a thousand times over. For so many years, I had held a stiltingly narrow view of God. I had a few words to define him—words like *friend, lover, parent*—that I could believe and embrace. And I had a few others—*omnipotent, mysterious, glorious*—that were pretty much names I only knew the intellectual meaning of.

As my husband once said about our past mind-set: "You could've asked me anything you wanted to know about God, and

I could've given you all the answers." All we had to do was pull out a few scriptures and there you had it. God.

The Jews, however, are enraptured by and comfortable with mystery. God pulsates with veiled secrets eagerly waiting to be disrobed. New surprises lie wrapped for discovery, like a box in which you find another box in which you find another box, ad infinitum. If one is knotted or taped too tightly, then the Jews keep at it until it yields. Or until it doesn't. Then they start all over again, probing, being surprised, finding new mysteries.

Acknowledging God as mystery allows you to experience God in new ways. God *is* still father and love and tenderness, but God is also creative energy, mother, intuition, lightning, fragrance, darkness, shadow, blinding sunlight, and a whispering breeze. Indeed, I no longer refer to God simply as God, but I call God by different names in order to invoke new images and to make new discoveries about this Being's nature. In doing this, I've felt God's presence more powerfully than ever before.

In an essay for *Mars Hill Review,* I once wrote this:

> Very early in the morning, a single ray of sun sprinkles into my bedroom, creating a wide beam of smoky light on the wall facing my bed, shimmering in mysterious patterns over a clear, stencil-like line of shadowed flowers, bushes and tree limbs. It is playful and beautiful, the shadows dodging and melting into one another until the sun comes fully up, illuminating my room and destroying the kaleidoscope of silhouettes.
>
> With the coming of full light, though, the play disappears, and so it is, I believe, in life and faith. The play is exciting stuff and the Jewish people . . . frolic in it, with God, with theology. They seem content with the ethereal wisps of shadow and light, full of movement and illusiveness, and they shun any pretense of having the security and comfort of full light.[11]

Mystery fills the Jewish heart and mind with excitement, and it has, over the past several years, begun to fill mine. Jews are unafraid of questions that have no clear answers. In fact, in Judaism, questions are as valuable as—or even more valuable— than answers. Jews relish questions.

This was illustrated to me again by Rabbi G. who, one evening, began talking excitedly about a twenty-volume set of books that a company had offered for sale. The books were a compilation of the wisdom of the Hasidic rabbis. Rabbi G. said he knew one person who had read nothing else but had gained a deep wisdom simply because the books were so mystical.

Because I thought that all of the books were available only in Hebrew, I asked the rabbi if there were plans to translate them. Three *had* been translated, he said, but it was very difficult because how do you translate mystery?

During other nights of study, the rabbi would sometimes pause at a passage in scripture and become animated, his eyes wide with excitement. "You can't translate this," he'd tell us, "and you can't even interpret it except in a mystical way. Ask anyone. Ask the most learned scholar, ask the tzaddik [holy man], and he'll have no answer."

Mystics of all religions agree readily with this sentiment. If the intellect can grasp and express and explain something, then it's a lower form of knowledge. True knowledge for the Hebrew mind and in the Hebrew language can only come with experience.

Indeed, knowledge *is* experience. Adam *knew* Eve and she conceived, scripture says. Knowing for the Hebrew isn't an intellectual exercise. It is uniting.

This kind of knowing isn't something you can wrestle with intellectually until the light comes on. Imagine, for instance, trying to explain love to someone who has never experienced it.

Intellectually, the person might have an inkling of what you're talking about because he can understand your words and put the concepts together. But talk to him again after he's fallen in love, and now he *understands*. He *knows*. He's experienced it.

One aspect of the Jewish love of mystery concerns what Jews consider God's most holy name: YHVH. Jews believe this Name is utterly sacred, and virtually no Jew I know, including the most liberal, pronounces it or writes it with vowels. Since I've been worshiping and studying with the Jews, I don't either.

Jewish tradition holds that only once a year, on Yom Kippur, the Day of Atonement, was the name uttered, and then only by the High Priest. When he did so, all those who stood near fell on their faces and, though the name was pronounced ten times during the ceremony, no one would remember the pronunciation after leaving the temple.

"To this day," writes Abraham Joshua Heschel, "the priests close their eyes when pronouncing the blessing, because when the Temple was in existence, they would utter the Ineffable Name . . . and the *Shechinah* would rest on their eyes. In remembrance thereof they close their eyes."[12]

The Zohar, which is the best-known kabbalistic text, along with the commentary that is usually included with it, has much to say about the name. It alone will be exalted in the time of the Messiah, teaches the Zohar. When it appears, the "formless and the void and the darkness disappear, and form, fulness, and light replace them. Each of its letters is symbolic, the letter's meaning, their unique combinations, even each one's individual design, and only the "Holy Living-Creatures understand [them]."[13]

As I'm writing these words, it's the Jewish month of *Tamuz,* meaning heat, alluding to the warmth of this time of year. However, because the psalmist also uses this metaphor to describe God's power, the tetragrammaton, YHVH, according to Jewish mysticism, is supposed to emit the greatest mystical strength during the month of *Tamuz.*

The Jewish avoidance of pronouncing YHVH, even adding vowels to it, reflects the mystery of God's spirit, an aspect of God that is as enigmatic as a breath. Just as we can't express what God is, neither can we put sound to this name of God. It's shrouded in unknowing, protected from the intellect, and clothed in secrecy.

Rabbi Kushner writes:

What's this God's name?
The sound of breathing.
What's this God say?
Only the softest, barely audible noise.
And what's this God look like?
Nothing!

(This comfort with mystery, Rabbi Kushner notes, might explain why there are so few Jews in the world.)[14]

The Jewish regard for this name can't be overemphasized. Once, while I was reading Tanakh, I came across a passage in Leviticus 24:14 that says that a "son of [an] Israelite woman *pronounced* [emphasis mine] the Name and blasphemed." When I looked this up in the Christian Old Testament, it read, "the Israelite woman's son blasphemed the Name in a curse." Very different implications.

I'm intrigued by this regard for a name. Few things in Judaism, it seems, hold only surface meaning, and it's this constant delving deeper that makes study and worship so rich. YHVH isn't a word by which to address God; it's a holy part of God's very being. It's the power of creation, a life-giving force, an emanation of holiness. For me, it's been still another opportunity to plunge into the mysteries of God.

Although this name has special significance, the Jews regard all names of God as holy. In fact, many Orthodox Jews don't discard anything with a name of God written on it. Some Jews believe this applies only to names written in Hebrew, but others apply this rule to all translations and names for God. This is why you might see "G-d" written in place of "God." When the name is written as "G-d," it allows a strictly observant Jew to discard the paper on which it's written.

In one of my folders is a handout from an Orthodox study I attended a few years ago. At the bottom, in bold print, are the words: "Likutei Peshatim has Torah content—please treat it respectfully."

I remember once asking an Orthodox Jew to write something for me and, though he did so out of courtesy, I realized later that his hesitation came from writing down something sacred and giving it to me, when I would probably, out of lack of understanding of their tradition, treat it disrespectfully.

Although the name YHVH is the only name that can't be pronounced, the Jews, or at least Orthodox Jews, are careful about using any name of God, orally or in writing, for fear of using it in vain. A CD I purchased several years back to help me learn some Jewish prayers said that, as you practice the prayers, you should insert *HASHEM* (literally, "The Name"), a sort of generic name for God, instead of any proper name of God used in the actual prayer. When you recite the prayer at the proper time and with the proper *kavanah*, or intent, you should then recite whatever proper name of God the prayer calls for, the CD explained.

One story illustrating this is about a young boy who asked his father, a rabbi, for an apple but was told he couldn't have one. The boy recited the appropriate blessing for receiving an apple, and the rabbi, who didn't want God's name to be used in vain, quickly gave the boy the apple.[15]

So what do Orthodox Jews do with material that *does* contain a name of God or Torah portion? Orthodox synagogues contain a *genizah* (a container made sacred by its contents) where these materials may accumulate for months or years. When the vessel is full, it's given a formal burial. Or the holy material may be placed in the casket of a great rabbi.

Rabbi Alan Lew, in his book *One God Clapping,* tells of the funeral of Zayde Isaac, the "grandfather rebbe." As his body was being taken down the streets of Borough Park, Lew writes, men came out of the yeshivas and synagogues and placed worn-out Torahs and prayers books in his casket.[16]

Respecting the mysteries of God propels us into the world of the sacred. We bow before the One whom we can never really understand. Everything related to this Holy Mystery is treated with respect and honor. For me, encountering the Jews' regard for whatever surrounds God brings my worship of him to an entirely new level. God is still my loving father-mother, but God is also an unfathomable mystery before whom I can best stand only in holy silence.

There's no bottom in God's ocean, I'm learning, no ceiling in God's sky. God is fathomless, endless, formless, and above my intellect and ability to know completely. God can't be boxed in or adequately described, the Jews have shown me. Rather, the quest to know him wondrously extends the mystery even further, making the journey all the more exciting.

Although I've always loved mystery, I never had much of it, before meeting the Jews, within my religion or experience of God. Now I do. I no longer value answers more than I do questions. I relish in unknowing. And I long to know the God who fills the earth with glory, with mystery, and with love.

CHAPTER FIVE

Women in Yarmulkes

It's Tuesday evening, and ten of us are sitting around a dining-room table preparing for our bi-weekly study session with Hesha. We won't begin for ten more minutes, so we spend some time getting to know one another. Rob, Mike's *chevruta,* tells me that he grew up in an Orthodox home but abandoned his faith as a teenager and had little to do with Judaism until he met Hesha. She put vibrancy in faith, he said, and shortly after he began attending Ruach Torah, he once again became an observant Jew.

Both of us eavesdrop on a conversation Hesha is having with the atheist man whom she calls the holy skeptic. His daughter, like Rob, has begun to find a new depth to her faith since becoming involved with Ruach Torah, and she's the one who brought him to the study. "You're here because this is the morning sickness of your spiritual birth," Hesha tells him.

Hesha refuses to take anything on a surface level, nor does she give simplistic answers to any questions. If we're having a problem "in one world," she says, "we should deal with it in one of the other worlds." For instance, if doubt is creeping in on an intellectual level, in the world of *beriyah*, go into the world of *atzilut* (spirit) or *yetzirah* (emotion) and test your doubt there.

Every ritual, in addition to its traditional meaning, Hesha infuses with practical meaning for our lives. During the lighting of the Sabbath candles, for instance, she tells anyone who needs more light in their lives to stand around the candles and to feel the light and warmth of God, which they represent. Ritual handwashing becomes a time for deep contemplation and a silence impregnated by holiness.

Hesha's warmth and openness fills whatever room she's in. Once, when Mike and I slipped in late to an event in which she was speaking, Hesha ran over and hugged us, even though she was already standing at the microphone getting ready to speak.

Another time, Mike had taken home Hesha's "purim grog-ger"—a noisemaker used during the holiday of Purim—to repair it for her. After a few hours in the garage, he had it in good shape, but as he bent over to put the finishing touches on it, his back suddenly gave out and Mike spent the next couple of weeks in agony. At the next Ruach Torah prayer service, when I returned the purim grogger to Hesha, I told her what had happened.

The next morning, Hesha left the following message on our voice mail:

> Hey, Mike and Mary, this is Hesha Abrams. Hey, Mike, when I heard the story from Mary, I felt *so* badly for you. There should be some kind of cosmic rule that when you're doing a mitzvah [fixing the purim grogger], you should be in a bubble of protection, don't you think? So the next time one of us talks with the Holy One, I think we should put that one out there.
>
> I'm so sorry that you're hurting. I'm thinking of you and I'm sending lots of good healing prayers to you. I wanted to call and give you a little love message, to say thank you *so* much for fixing

my purim grogger! I was so ecstatic. I *love* that thing and you made it so much more beautiful and so much more perfect. I felt like it was a love gift to me. It was so sweet and beautiful and I wanted to thank you for that, and offer you a *bracha* for healing.

Hesha closed her message with an offer to courier Mike a pile of books, in case he was still laid up with his back. "Give me a call and let me know how you're doing because I'm worried about you and I'd feel better if I talked to you. Lots of blessings to you. Bye."

Hesha is one of my favorite women in yarmulkes. She's one of the most vibrant spiritual leaders I've ever met, and during the years that Ruach Torah gathered for prayer and study, I always left her presence feeling closer to God. There was a spiritual energy that remained with me, literally, for days. And I learned, from her example, how to stand back from the cares of the world and to bask in the spiritual ambiance and drama that I've come to realize is always taking place within and around me.

Like other Jewish women, Hesha has struggled with what is sometimes seen as conflicting desires in Judaism—to serve God in a leadership position yet to remain faithful to *halakhah*, or Jewish law. Hesha would have loved to train as a rabbi at an Orthodox or Hasidic yeshiva, but they don't admit women for rabbinical training. And she had other problems with the more liberal Jewish seminaries.

"Jewish Renewal?" she wondered. At first, she had a problem with this, also. "I'm an attorney," she told me. "I'm used to going to school and getting into intense academic studies. In Jewish Renewal, you have teachers and mentors, but you don't have traditional classroom study. You do it on your own." In the end, though, that seemed the best option for her, and she began the process of becoming a Jewish Renewal rabbi.

As I've gotten to know Hesha and other "women in yarmulkes," I've often resonated with their thoughts and experiences as women struggling to find a place in a historically patriarchal religion. Yet I also fully understand the beliefs and feelings of Orthodox women. Indeed, with each female Jewish friend I've made, regardless of their ideology, I've been astonished by how much we, in many ways, have in common.

Although no one explanation encompasses the feminine perspective in Orthodox Judaism, it's safe to say that in the mainstream, it's unacceptable for women to study to become rabbis or cantors. In addition, women aren't "called to Torah," that is, they don't read Torah during the prayer services.

Not long ago, I had lunch with an Orthodox woman, Pam Fine, and I mentioned her synagogue—the first Orthodox synagogue besides Chabad that I'd attended. I asked her how she felt about "sitting on the side," not being allowed to participate fully in the prayer service or to hold an ordained, leadership position.

Pam looked surprised. "I don't think we even feel put on the side," she replied. "It's just separate, and I don't know any Orthodox women who don't prefer that. Maybe we've just chosen that, or we're used to it."

As we talked, I remembered attending a Traditional synagogue with a couple of married friends who, although space was provided for them to sit together, chose to pray on opposite sides of the synagogue, in the "men only" and "women only" sections. This was what Pam was talking about; for some, it's a preference.

Pam explained to me that for many women in Orthodox Judaism, life isn't about going to synagogue. "It isn't the most important thing," she said. "It's once a week. Spirituality, on the other hand, is something we do every minute of the day." When I pressed her about her feelings about being forbidden to read Torah or hold public leadership positions, she shook her head. "I don't have a need for public expression," she said. "I can see how it would be frustrating to a woman who does, but I don't."

Frequently I've been told that, as an outsider, I wouldn't understand the feelings of Orthodox Jewish women, but this is entirely wrong. The various beliefs that underlie the roles of women in Judaism are very similar, if not identical, to those in Christianity, and I've been in virtually all of those roles at different periods of my life.

Orthodox Jewish women want to follow *halakhah* and, for them, following it means adhering to a traditional interpretation of canonical texts; women have a role to play in their religion, but it isn't leading a prayer service. In the conservative churches of which I was once a part, we also believed that women played an important role in the life of religion, but it wasn't in becoming a pastor or holding leadership roles that put women in the pulpit. The reason was basically the same: we interpreted scripture—our "law"—as stating that women had different roles to play in the life of the church.

A few years ago, I attended an Orthodox service in which a young woman was to become a bat mitzvah, a coming-of-age ceremony for Jewish women (young men become *bar* mitzvah). In this synagogue, women sat on each side of the sanctuary in "rooms" that one entered through doors other than the ones the men used.

After the prayer service, however, the entire sanctuary buzzed noisily as the women moved into the main sanctuary. The room became divided, with men sitting on one side of the sanctuary and the women seated on the other, though a number of men, apparently the stricter Orthodox, moved to the "side rooms" to maintain a higher degree of separation. After a few minutes, the bat mitzvah service began.

The young woman, Sarah, was awesome. After the rabbi spoke, Sarah read her Torah portion from the Hebrew scroll, then gave a dynamic twenty-minute sermon. She was honored to become a bat mitzvah, she said, on the week before Rosh Chodesh—a holiday that, in part, commemorates the women who refused to donate their gold earrings to Aaron for the construction of the idol, which had been made in desperation over Moses' lengthy stay on Mount Sinai.

"The women are honored during this time as more spiritual and righteous than the men," Sarah said. The men responded enthusiastically, listening attentively, breaking into song every once in a while, shouting words of encouragement. Afterward, the rabbi moved back to the podium and praised the content of her message, saying it was as deep as it was wide. She would go to Harvard or Columbia, he said, because she was so intelligent and eloquent.

Initially, I was amazed by what seemed such a paradox: women forbidden an active part of the prayer service but so honored in this important ceremony, which had been for many years also denied women. But again, all I needed to do was travel back in my own memory a decade or so.

Likewise, after prayer services in my former churches were over, men and women became "equals." We studied and argued over our sacred texts, and I rarely, if ever, felt any disdain or discrimination from the Christian men who forbade me leadership positions in the church. In our minds, we were merely following what we believed to be God's design for men and women in our religion. And that morning, as I sat perplexed by the bat mitzvah service at the Orthodox synagogue, I reminded myself of what I, too, had once believed.

Although I'm no longer comfortable with the "separate but equal" theology of any religion, Judaism has, in some ways, shed some light on passages in the Bible that have troubled me over the years. One of these is the Sotah ritual (Numbers 5:11–31), in which a woman accused of adultery is brought before the *kohen* (priest) and made to drink water, which will curse her if she's guilty of adultery.

I remember once, during a particularly trying time in my life, when I came across this passage and it almost turned me entirely against religion—at least any religion that used the Bible. Although I came through it after finding a new church, it wasn't until much later that I learned how the ritual played out in practical Jewish life.

For one thing, in order for the woman to have been brought to the priest in the first place, a reliable witness must have seen the woman enter a closed room with a specific man for a specific amount of time, and her husband must have warned her in advance not to be with this man. The ritual, it's said, was enacted to diffuse jealousy by removing the matter from a jealous husband's hands. The Torah was merely trying to save women's lives in the only way it could at the time.

Although this isn't entirely consoling to me (no woman could bring her husband to the priest if she suspected *him,* and women were almost always punished more harshly than were men for sexual misconduct), this at least softened the nastiness of a superficial reading.

As I've struggled with the patriarchal laws and stories in scripture, however, I've also noticed those men who, in some ways, rose above the mentality of their era. Many of the greatest men who appear in the Bible deeply loved and esteemed their wives, often obeying them. When Sarah demanded that Hagar be sent away, for instance, Abraham obeyed, even when it broke his heart to do so. Jacob worked fourteen years to win a single woman, and Adam, representative of mankind, was given the entire earth and every beautiful thing that sprang from its womb, yet felt incomplete and unhappy until he was given a female companion.

Mystical Judaism has a number of lovely midrashim about the value of women. One of my favorites is a story in which it's said that one thousand years after Rachel died, the Jews put an idol in the temple and that, for punishment, God planned to place them in permanent exile.

Although the soul of Abraham rose up and pleaded with God, reminding God that he had brought monotheism to the world, God wouldn't listen. So Isaac's soul stood before God, playing on the merit of his willingness to be sacrificed. But still God's anger flared. Jacob appeared before God, then Moses and many others, but God continued to insist on exiling his people.

Finally, Rachel's soul presented itself to God. She began,

> Master of the Universe, I waited seven years to marry my beloved Jacob. When the time of the wedding finally came, my father schemed to switch me with my sister Leah. Jacob suspected this would happen, so together we made up a password. But I realized that Leah would be put to shame if the scheme were uncovered, so I had compassion for my sister and gave her the password. I overcame my own feelings and was not jealous. I allowed a competitor into my home. So if I was able to do it, God, then all the more so You too should not be exacting of the idol—the competitor in Your home.

Immediately, God's compassion was aroused. He said, "Don't cry over the exile, Rachel, because for your sake I will in the future return the children of Israel to their homeland once again."[1]

Jewish women have, in these ways, helped me re-imagine scripture. Not long ago, I attended a women's study led by an interesting rabbi, Debra Robbins, at Temple Emanu-El. Although Rabbi Robbins grew up in a religious family—both her parents and grandparents were active in their Reform congregations—Rabbi Robbins was the first in her family to become a rabbi. And this happened, despite the fact that, as she was growing up, she had never met a female rabbi.

Rabbi Robbins was ordained eleven years ago and has served since that time at Temple Emanu-El, which employs five full-time rabbis and a Rabbi Emeritus. Rabbi Robbins leads services, makes herself accessible to any of the thirty-five hundred families who are members there, visits the sick, counsels, and involves herself in various community affairs. This year, as Senior Rabbi David Stern took a seven-month sabbatical, Rabbi Robbins stepped in as acting senior rabbi—a daunting task but one she approached with eagerness, confidence, and proficiency.

At any rate, the text we delved into at our study was *The Women's Torah Commentary,* a compilation of studies and reflections on the Torah written entirely by female rabbis.[2] *"Baruch ata Adonai, Ehloheinu mehlech haolam . . . ,"* we said before our study began: "Blessed is the Eternal, our God, Ruler of the Universe, who sanctifies our lives through mitzvot and commands us to engage in the study of Torah."

What was interesting to me, though, was Rabbi Robbins's mixed feelings about teaching this group. "If we really believe we're egalitarian, that boys and girls should have bar or bat mitzvahs at age thirteen, that men and women can serve in all leadership roles in the congregation, then to create things that are exclusively for women is very problematic for me," she explained. But she continues to do so because "it fills a need."

Rabbi Robbins believes that the more talk there is about women rabbis, the more attention we draw to the "women" part of it. "I'm waiting for the day, Mary, when I'm just a rabbi," Rabbi Robbins told me.

Again, I resonated with her feelings. It had been less than a decade since I'd left a church that excluded women from ordained leadership positions. When I left, I became the Dallas–Fort Worth president of a large evangelical organization that worked to change the way churches interpreted scripture regarding women and thus tried to move toward a more egalitarian church in general.

After becoming involved with a new church that encouraged the full participation of women, however, I no longer felt a need to be involved with the organization. I came to believe that you should just go where you're accepted. Like Rabbi Robbins, I believed that women and men should work in partnership and that the focus shouldn't be primarily on *women* but on women's *ministry.*

Yet I continue to vacillate. Surely we still need a feminine emphasis. Can we possibly have overcome so many hundreds of years of patriarchy in a few short decades? Is there really no need to focus specifically on women and women's issues and feminine perspectives?

My friend Karen Prager points out that in the history of the women's liberation movement, advances have always been made when women band together and become passionate for some area of change. It's only after this initial coming together of women, she says, that the men usually join us and further the cause.

Not only this but women often need their own groups to discuss issues and life changes that only other women truly understand. When the Women's Rabbinic Network (WRN) became solidified, for instance, they discussed whether it should remain an all-women's organization. The answer came when a male rabbi tried to join and the WRN promptly returned his check. Female rabbis, they decided, needed a "haven" where they could openly discuss issues that centered around their unique concerns and challenges as female rabbis.[3]

"During the early stirrings of the feminist movement," writes Carole B. Balin in a prologue to an issue of a rabbinical journal issued to celebrate twenty-five years of women in the rabbinate, "women rediscovered the bonding between members of their own sex that had been the special resource and strength of many generations before them."[4]

Recently, I began attending a Rosh Chodesh group at Karen's invitation. In ancient times, Judaism as a whole celebrated this holiday—a day that coincides with the new moon and thus the Jewish calendar. Although the holiday fell by the wayside for hundreds of years, Jewish feminist groups have recently resurrected it, as the moon is a reflection of the cycles of women's lives.

Roz Katz, who leads the group, puts together, with the help of other members, something different for each monthly meeting. The group may discuss new, meaningful rituals for women, watch a film designed to generate discussion about a current interest, or examine a piece of Judaic literature with the aim of a fresh, feminine understanding. But spirituality and female bonding are at the heart of all Rosh Kodesh groups.

I've also been enriched by Hesha's incorporation of the feminine into holiday services. One of these was the festival of Sukkot, in which Jews celebrate the harvest and remember their ancestors who once lived in the desert under a roof of stars. Of all degrees of joy felt during this season, say the Jewish sages, Sukkot possesses the most intense.

During Sukkot, many Jews build a *sukkah,* or hut, in their backyard; observant Jews sleep and eat their meals here for seven days. On the festival day, about thirty of us gathered inside Jeff and Hesha's *sukkah.* Several candles flickered as Hesha instructed us to quietly gaze up at the stars, thinking of the abundance with which we're surrounded. Fruit and vegetables dangled from the rafters, and various Jewish blessings, which Hesha had written and attached to the walls, surrounded us.

Later, when I wrote of our celebration for Ruach Torah's newsletter, I remembered Hesha's instructions to mystically invite the matriarchs as well as the patriarchs to our gathering:

> "I invite Esther," said one person, "because I admire her courage." "I invite Joseph for his integrity," said another. Ruth entered the Sukkah, bringing with her the quality of loyalty. And David, with his soulful and passionate love, came, invited by me. Mystically, the room filled with holy people and we sat quietly, absorbing their strengths.

For Passover, Hesha again introduced some egalitarian aspects to the traditional seder, which began at 6:30 in the evening and concluded around 1 A.M. As we read the traditional Haggadah, Hesha paused at each part, saying, "yeah, yeah, that's what it means on a *'peshat'* [superficial or literal] level, but what does it mean in the world of *atzilut* [the highest, mystical realm where we encounter union with God]?"

Though *dayeanu* ("it is enough") is traditionally sung at seders, Hesha decided we weren't going to sing it at our mystical seder because, "let's face it, let's be honest, it's never enough; we'll always want more." Instead, we went around the room, stating the one thing we wanted most in the world. "Don't be overly spiritual," said Hesha, "be truthful. Be in the world of *yetzirah,* in the heart, where we're most open and sincere."

During our seder, we took turns reading drashes (stories and sayings) that Hesha had compiled and that were designed to help us become more satisfied and content with our lives.

The feminine touch to the service came after we had passed around the traditional cup of Elijah, who is said to be mystically present at the seder (an empty chair is set up for him and the front door left open). After this cup was passed, however, we also passed a cup for Miriam.

I've read some on this practice. In the late 1970s, a small group of women began rewriting Haggadah to include the matriarchs and to address women's specific needs and concerns. According to rabbinic tradition, Miriam located wells for the Israelites during their desert journeys. The seder cup symbolizes and memorializes her for her actions.

Some egalitarian seders also include the midwives Shifra and Puah, who refused to comply with the Pharaoh's order to kill Hebrew male infants. Haggadahs urge Jews not to forget that their ancestors were saved through the brave actions of two women: one Hebrew and one Egyptian—Miriam and the daughter of Pharaoh.

I had never been in groups led by women or consisting entirely of women who were interested in bringing a feminine perspective to God and to scripture. It was refreshing and enlightening. It broadened my vision of God and put a new twist on biblical stories and characters. I loved it.

One of these twists again comes from Karen Prager. Although the Shekhinah hasn't always been seen as a feminine aspect of God, mystical Judaism began speaking of it in this manner several hundred years ago, and Jewish feminists have picked up on it. The Shekhinah, or Presence of God, says Karen, lost Her home in the Temple when it was destroyed, and has since then wandered with the Jewish people. *Shekhinah,* she adds, is a grammatically feminine term meaning "she who dwells."

There's a yearning in the "inner life of Godde," Karen wrote me some years back (she uses the term *Godde* to remind us that God is neither [or both] masculine or feminine but is both god and goddess), and it's the tzaddik's job to bring about the union of the Shekhinah and the Tiferet (foundation). Although not all Jews regard the Shekhinah in feminine terms, some have found in it an additional resource for connection to and expression of the feminine aspects of a God who has historically been referred to solely with masculine terminology.

Commenting on the practice of re-imagining God, Neil Gillman writes, "The process of creating new images of God never ends as long as there are people who continue to experience God's presence in their lives and to reflect on that experience." God's "intrinsic unknowability," he tells us, freed the ancient Jews and it can, as well, free us today to "reach into the core of our own experiences of God and to fashion the widest possible range of images to capture."[5]

These are such lovely thoughts and experiences for me. In my not-so-distant past, I, along with the churches I attended, feared seeing God as feminine, even while we hurried to add that God wasn't male. Translations of scripture that used feminine—or even inclusive—pronouns angered us because we believed that this was somehow actually changing God.

No one, however, is changing God. We're merely expanding our *images* of God. Using feminine imagery helps us, in part, to feel the motherly aspects of God: nurturing and tenderness and emotion. It helps us grow spiritually, giving us new experiences of God as we "re-imagine" this Being that, in some sense, defies our very imagination.

One of my Jewish friends recently told me that she quit going to synagogue because she had grown tired of the patriarchal tone of her religion. She indicated to me that she believed Judaism to be alone in its history of male dominance. Clearly, this isn't the truth. It has only been in recent years, for instance, and particularly in the West, that women have become Buddhist monks. Nor do we ever hear of female reincarnations of the Dalai Lama. Although I've studied numerous cultures around the world, female dominance is virtually unheard of.

The female gods of the Greeks, regardless of the power they bore and the fact that they were considered gods at all, were always subordinate to male gods. In the Celtic religion, attempts to prove that the Druids (the Celtic priesthood) had women in their ranks are weak. "The Druids no more had women in their ranks," writes Douglas Monroe, "than the Catholic Church has had over the last 2000 years. Women shamans they may have been, prophets and healers—but they were not *Druids*."[6]

What this woman failed to realize is that virtually *all* religions share a similar past but that most are now experiencing a transformation in their view of women and their roles in leadership. There are places of worship in Judaism, as well as in Christianity, that simply regard traditionally off-limit roles and positions as an acceptable non-issue.

Last year, I received an invitation to attend my friend Karen's bat mitzvah. I was surprised by the invitation, as Karen was one of the most knowledgeable people I knew regarding Judaism. Surely, I thought, she'd grown up attending Hebrew school, faithful to a synagogue, and familiar from her childhood with the religion in which she was so intimately involved.

All of my assumptions, I later found out, were indeed true. Karen *had* grown up attending synagogue and Hebrew school. Her parents, while ideologically liberal, were active, religious Jews. It wasn't common, however, when Karen was growing up, for Jewish women to go through the coming-of-age ceremony that all boys went through. She had never had a bat mitzvah ceremony.

As Karen grew up, she turned against her faith, becoming an atheist. She threw herself into her career, earning a Ph.D., taking a position as professor at a respected university, and opening a small counseling practice. However, she knew something was missing in her life, and she eventually began her journey back to faith in God and to the faith with which she'd grown up: Judaism.

Karen's return was one of great enthusiasm. She began intensive studies of Judaism, of Hebrew, of Jewish feminism, and of the rituals of her faith. For her bat mitzvah, she began studying with a friend so she could chant Torah. With the help of her rabbis and mentors, she wrote her entire two-hour ceremony and had it beautifully illustrated and bound for the congregation to use as we followed the service.

During Karen's first Torah reading, or *aliyah* as it's traditionally called, her family stood around her, and her lovely voice rose and fell in the melodic cadence of the chant. For the second *aliyah,* she called her mentors to stand with her. She also chanted a *haftorah* portion (a section of the Bible, outside the Torah, which is also read each Sabbath).

Karen told her story of her return to God and to Judaism. Pausing to stifle a sob and looking around as if she might see her deceased mother watching in spirit, Karen said she knew her mom was with God and that she would have been proud. As for herself, Karen said, she was just "dancing with the knowledge of how much she loved God." At the conclusion of the service, Karen stood with Rabbi David Stern before the ark and he, gripping her shoulders, delivered a blessing.

"I've been to hundreds of bar and bat mitzvahs," said the woman beside me, "but that was the most beautiful."

As we filed out of the sanctuary, Karen seemed to be floating on clouds. Many of her friends present that day had seen her turn from atheism to a woman infused with spiritual fervor.

Why had she returned? For one thing, upon Karen's willingness to look again into her own faith she discovered that her denomination was returning to the richness of ritual, that it was reincorporating the Hebrew language into the prayer service, and that the people there worshiped with hearts filled with vitality and love.

Yet this same faith was increasingly opening its doors, fully, to women. It was re-imagining God and embracing new images that reflected God's feminine aspects. New songs were being written, new prayers and blessings, and even new rituals—all of which made women feel a more intimate part of religious life and worship.

For me, this is enchanting. After spending more than three decades with a single view of God, I'm now seeing a new face of God, thanks to the Jewish women with whom I've worshiped and studied. And it's a God who not only honors a woman's desire to serve in whatever ways she feels led but a God who, in many ways, reflects the essence of her very being. What an astounding vision that has been for me as a woman.

CHAPTER SIX

Men in Black Hats

Having been invited to attend a Purim party at Rabbi G.'s home a few years ago, I was brimming with excitement. Hasidic celebrations are always wild and joyful, with plenty of dancing and laughter, and I love attending them. When I arrived at this one, however, I was a bit startled to find that I was one of only two people not from Russia—and the only one speaking English.

Men and women filled every inch of the living room and spilled down both hallways, straining to listen to the rabbi as he read the Megillah—the story of Esther—from a kosher scroll. Purim is the Jewish holiday that celebrates the defeat of Haman, the evil king's aide who was plotting to kill the Jews. Mordechai, however—the cousin who had adopted Esther when she was a child—heard about the plot and gave the information to her. Queen Esther then approached her husband, the king, to plead for the Jews' lives, even though her bold approach could have cost her her own life.

For the Jews, Purim is a holiday of great joy, a celebration of saved life. It's also the Jewish holiday in which it's a mitzvah to get drunk. Although most Jews don't, most Hasidim do. At an earlier study, when someone mentioned Purim, jokingly saying they'd be allowed to get drunk, Rabbi G. had said, "Not that you can; you must." Talmud states that "a person should drink on Purim until the point where they can't tell the difference between 'Blessed is Mordechai' and 'Cursed is Haman.'"

After the reading of the story of Esther, everyone rushed to one of several white-clothed tables set up in the dining room. I stood in a corner, hoping I'd hear someone speaking English, but I didn't, so I finally chose a table at random. Giant bowls of slaw were being passed around, and the man next to me heaped some onto my plate. He also poured me a large glass of wine. Then, to my surprise, he began speaking English. Indeed, for the remainder of the evening, he translated everything the rabbi and others said. I was thrilled.

Men and women poured from the kitchen with mountains of food and, accompanied by a live singer, we dug in. Bottles of sweet kosher wine flooded the tables, along with vodka; when my glass got even a tad low, someone at my table promptly filled it up. The man next to me continually ladled food onto my plate.

As the party got under way, Rabbi G. gestured for the man who had been robustly entertaining the crowd with klezmer music to give up his microphone. As the rabbi took his place behind the microphone, he tried to hush the noisy crowd, but no one heard him. "Shh, shh!" Rabbi G. said. "I have something *mystical* to tell you!" The crowd continued their animated and noisy conversation. Rabbi G. tried again. "Be quiet because I have something *mystical* to tell you!"

Suddenly, another Hasidic rabbi jumped to his feet and began dancing a slow, circular dance around his chair. He raised both hands in the air as he danced, his *kippah* sliding off his head as someone jumped to retrieve it for him. "Let's—get—mystical!" he shouted.

Grinning, Rabbi G. politely waited for the rabbi to re-seat himself, and then he tried again. "Friends!" he said, "I have something to tell you about *God!* Be quiet! I have something to tell you about *God!*"

At another table, a third Hasidic rabbi leapt to his feet and lifted his arms, his voice drowning out the crowd. "Let's—talk—about—God!" he shouted.

With everyone now more animated than ever, Rabbi G. gave up on bringing us his brief, mystical talk. Shoving tables against the wall, the men suddenly began congregating in the middle of the room, dancing exuberantly, and singing. Someone hoisted one of the rabbis onto his shoulders as the others lifted their feet in traditional Jewish dance. The singer resumed his place at the microphone.

As the men abandoned themselves to the joy of their holiday, the man sitting next to me asked me to dance with him. I explained it wasn't allowed for men and women to dance together. He called Boris over—a prominent man in Rabbi G.'s synagogue—and asked him, in Russian, what would happen if we danced anyway, even if it was forbidden. (Boris later told me what he had asked, and I assured him that although I had made plenty of faux pas, that was certainly one I knew not to make.) Thankfully, the man hadn't pushed it; however, he did admit he "just couldn't buy into everything Orthodox Judaism forbids."

I can't either. But of all the varieties of Judaism and Jews I've been around—a considerable number by this time—I love the Hasidim most of all. Rabbi G. is one of the most fascinating teachers I've ever sat under. He exudes kindness and humility and makes each of his students feel special, encouraging them in whatever steps they take to become more observant, no matter how small that step is.

Indeed, the Hasidim in general captivate me. Although many Jews study mysticism, the Hasidim *live* it. Everything—every verse in scripture, the smallest events in everyday life, the tiniest aspect of creation—has mystical meaning. Whatever they do for God, they believe, must have heart and *kavanah* (intent), and they constantly look for ways to infuse each ritual and action with deep devotion. They readily admit this isn't possible to do perfectly, but that doesn't stop them from trying.

Their worship services are emotional and fervent, although this varies from group to group and with individual synagogues. I'll never forget one service I attended in Colorado, led by several Hasidim from Jerusalem and New York. Early in the morning in one member's home, several men and women erected a *mechitza,* and about two dozen men and women gathered to pray. Someone pulled the drapes as the sun began to burst over the mountains. I sat quietly with my eyes closed, absorbing the sound of prayer and feeling the intense presence of God.

Suddenly, however, the room grew very still. It was a quietness, not just in absence of sound but in a way that reminded me of the "still small voice of God," a stillness that grips your heart and fills you with awe. I remembered reading once that composers put a moment of quiet into their music before launching into the most dramatic part. This is what that morning felt like—a silent moment of intense anticipation.

In the next breath, the room filled with the sound of the *Shema. "Shema Israel, Adonai Ehloheinu, Adonai Echod"* ("Hear, O Israel, the Lord is our God, the Lord is One!").

The men and women voiced the prayer with passion, every voice blending together, each word spoken by everyone at precisely the same moment, as if they had rehearsed it together for months. Spontaneously, I dropped my head, afraid to look up, so powerful was the presence of God.

Moments with the Hasidim, however holy, are rarely this quiet. The Hasidim are known more for their emotional outpouring and their exuberance, though again, different sects, as well as individuals, have their own personalities. Indeed, the primary reason Hasidism formed was to infuse passion, emotion, and heartfelt intent into Jewish ritual at a time when it had become automatic and virtually spiritless within the general community.

"The founder of modern Hasidism, Israel Baal Shem Tov . . . breathed life into a Judaism that had become ossified with punctilious observance of ritual and devoid of any emotional content," writes Robert Eisenberg, "and his influence spread to millions of Jews over the next two centuries."[1]

Typically, stories of Hasidic fervor abound. Ben Birnbaum, in an article for *Image* journal, writes of Rav Moshe of Kobrin, who "in reciting the preamble to just about every Jewish blessing— 'Blessed art thou, Lord our God'—cried out 'blessed' with such fervor that he had to sit and rest before he could continue with 'art thou.'" Birnbaum also writes of the Koznitzer Maggid, who danced on the table during worship.[2]

Elie Wiesel, as always, brims with stories about the emotional fervor of the Hasidim. The Great Maggid of Mezeritch, Wiesel writes, claimed that the dancing of his Hasidim counted for more than his own prayers. He was the first, says Wiesel, to turn dance into ritual.

One Hasidic rabbi worshiped with such abandon, Wiesel tells us, that his "frightened faithful instinctively moved away. He gesticulated, howled and danced, jumping from one corner to the other, pushing and overturning whatever was in his way."[3] One rebbe sometimes went to theaters and taverns because he "enjoyed their atmosphere," which was one of gaiety and uninhibited hilarity.[4] Another claimed that it was possible to usher in the age of the Messiah through the power of dance.[5]

Passionate expression is called for in every action, each mitzvah, every moment of prayer and worship. The body, the Hasidim believe, should accompany the soul in coming alive in God's presence. This isn't, however, merely an emotional frenzy. There's an intimate communion with God and his law behind these passionate expressions of joy. The Hasidim have the highest regard for study, and they're meticulous observers of Jewish law.

Although emotional displays can sometimes be superficial, there is nothing superficial about the Hasidim. For them, few things are worse than merely going through the motions of religion. Burning and fire, Rabbi G. has said, take us to the next "portal" in drawing closer to God. Opening the heart is done by passion and love, and for a Hasid, this opening is the only way to truly experience God.

I've always believed that love should be full of passion and heartfelt expression, though it's sometimes difficult to feel such intensity for a Being that isn't physically present. When I'm with the Hasidim, however, I become caught up in their utter devotion to God. This isn't a passing emotion that's worked up during a celebration then disappears afterward; it's a release of love and joy that they work toward feeling each moment of their lives. That's a lifestyle I long to emulate.

The Hasidic movement began in Poland-Lithuania in the late eighteenth century, seeking to ignite the Jewish love of study and observance of the law with intense emotion and fervent prayer. The Hasidim's study of Torah is accompanied by an immersion in various Jewish mystical texts, and the mysterious meanings of these infuse each story and dogma in the Hebrew Bible.

The Lubavitchers (a prominent Hasidic sect throughout the world and the one with which I've studied most regularly) focus on a kabbalistic text called the Tanya, written by the founder of the Lubavitcher movement, Rebbe Shneur-Zalmen of Ladi (1747–1813). A more familiar kabbalistic text is the Zohar, a sacred text to all Hasidim, but also a popular book studied by Jews and non-Jews in New Age types of settings.

The Baal Shem Tov—literally, Master of the Good Name—founded Hasidism after claiming to have received a revelation in the 1730s. After his death, another great leader, Dov Baer of Mezhirech, continued to spread the teachings of Hasidism. As the movement became more and more popular, sects sprang up led by charismatic, holy men called rebbes, usually identified by the town from which they came.

A rebbe is a "spiritual master" and not necessarily a rabbi, though he sometimes is (or was). "A rabbi is a scholar of Jewish law who acquires his knowledge and authority through 'left-brain' book learning," writes Rabbi Yonassan Gershom, a Hasid from the Breslover sect. "A Rebbe is a saintly mystic who also understands the various levels of the soul, can read people's reincarnations, advise them about their spiritual life, etc."[6]

Rebbes are almost always larger than life, and tales of miracles surround them. One rebbe was said to be able to know a man's sins by looking at his forehead. "One day," writes Wiesel, "the faithful appeared at the synagogue with their caps pulled way down to their eyebrows." The rebbe's response? "You really believe that a garment can prevent my eyes from seeing?" he asked them.[7]

In *Chasidic Stories Made in Heaven,* published by the Lubavitchers, a Hasid tells a story to illustrate that a rebbe "never makes mistakes." A "simple Jew" named Chaim Zelig, "honest and decent," rented and operated an inn from the local *poretz,* or landlord. Zelig and his family also lived on the property. If peasants ordered a glass of vodka, they knew they would get a glass of vodka, not a watery mixture. Whenever someone ran short on cash, Zelig would extend them credit; furthermore, he would never pressure them to pay their bills.

Although he had always been well liked by the *poretz,* one day he was called into his office and told he would have to vacate the property. Zelig, shocked and devastated, pressed the inn's owner to reconsider his decision, but the man wouldn't budge from his decision. Nor would he give Zelig a reason why he was evicting him.

In desperation, Zelig appealed to his rebbe. As he entered the "holy chambers," Zelig burst into tears, asking for his rebbe's advice and wondering aloud if the rebbe might write a letter to a rich Hasid named Berel the Short. Because of Berel's stature in the community, Zelig said, he might be able to persuade the *poretz* to reconsider his decision.

The rebbe agreed that this might help, and he immediately wrote the letter, placed it in an envelope, and handed it to Zelig, who went hopefully on his way. A bit later, however, Zelig happened to look down at the envelope and found, to his horror, that it had been written to the wrong person! It was addressed to a man known as Berel the Tall, a teacher of young children, "oblivious to the intricacies of finance." He would be no help to Zelig at all!

Zelig was agitated. He certainly couldn't return to the rebbe announcing that he had made a mistake. Heaven forbid. In fact, it would be unlikely that he would even be allowed another audience with the holy man. Finally, he decided to approach one of the rebbe's sons. But when Zelig told the son the story, the rebbe's son was indignant. "My father does not make mistakes!" he exclaimed. "If he addressed the letter to Berel the Tall, it is meant for Berel the Tall."

Instead of agitating Zelig further, the son's confidence in his father filled Zelig with hope. He set out for the town where Berel the Tall lived and, upon finding him at home, handed him the letter. When Berel realized that Zelig was holding a letter from the rebbe, he ran to wash his hands and put on a holy garment called a *gartel.* But after reading the letter, Berel could only assure Zelig that he was indeed in trouble and that he didn't see how help could come through him.

Nonetheless, he told Zelig, the rebbe can "see from one end of the world to the other and knows the future. If we truly believe in the Rebbe's powers we will merit a salvation that transcends mere nature. Strengthen yourself, my brother," he said, "for it will surely come. You are welcome to stay in my house until it arrives."

A room was prepared for Zelig, and he settled in. Days passed and Zelig struggled to have faith. Then one evening a terrible storm blew through the area. In the middle of the night, Zelig was awakened by a loud banging on the door. When he opened it, there stood the *poretz,* drenched from the pounding rain and shivering with cold. Zelig, whom the *poretz* didn't recognize, ran to wake Berel.

Berel opened his home to the *poretz,* throwing logs on the fire, preparing food and a warm drink for him, and gave him a dry change of clothes. The next morning, after the storm had passed, the *poretz* prepared to return to his home, but first he asked Berel how he could pay him back for his kindness. "Ask of me whatever you wish," the *poretz* said. "I am a wealthy man, and will gladly fulfill your request."

115

At first Berel refused any kind of payment, explaining to the *poretz* that being able to fulfill the mitzvah of hospitality was enough reward, but the *poretz* insisted, so Berel asked that he renew the inn's lease for his friend Zelig. The *poretz* gladly agreed.

Later, as Zelig signed the agreement, he couldn't resist asking the *poretz* why he had evicted him in the first place. The *poretz* explained that a man had recently approached him with the news that his brother-in-law had lost everything in a fire and asked that Zelig be evicted so the inn could be run by his unfortunate family member. The *poretz* told Zelig that the man requesting this favor was wealthy and that the *poretz* had, on occasion, borrowed money from him. Thus, he didn't see how he could refuse the man's request. However, to repay Berel, who opened his home to him during the storm, he had now changed his mind. The wealthy man's name? Berel the Short.

"How true were the words of the rebbe's son when he said, 'My father does not make mistakes!'" cried Zelig, throwing his arms around Berel the Tall.[8]

Legends and stories surround almost all great rebbes. In *Hasidic Tales of the Holocaust,* Yaffa Eliach writes that "the Hasidic storyteller has unlimited options open to him, including sources based in folklore and humor. Hasidism imposes no restrictions on its storytellers. For a creative mind within a religious movement, this is an extraordinary and very welcome freedom, almost without parallel in the literature of other religious movements."[9] However, one shouldn't think that all extraordinary tales are untrue. For who's to say what miraculous connections holy men (tzaddiks) have with the spiritual world?

Growing up and long into my adult years, I rejected the idea that some people were holier than others. In my religious tradition, saints were people Catholics revered. As a Protestant, I didn't need anyone to pray for me, especially someone who was dead. Now,

however, I'm fascinated by extraordinarily holy people. I fully realize that there are people who are so devoted to God that just by
being near them I'm absorbing the Holy Being whom they radiate.
In Judaism, the rebbes aren't just spiritual leaders; they're great
saints who frequently touched the throne of God, and their passion
for God astounds and motivates me.

Eliach relates another story that is heartbreaking but inspiring, illustrating the great love and respect, even awe and wonder,
that Hasidim have for their rebbes. In "Hovering Above the Pit,"
Eliach tells the following tale.

> One late, cold night at the Janowska Road [Concentration] Camp,
> the prisoners were suddenly awakened and thrust in the direction
> of an open field. Gasping for breath and stumbling across the
> dark field, the men and women found themselves standing before
> two giant pits. In horror, they realized what was about to occur.
>
> "Each of you dogs who values his miserable life and wants to
> cling to it," screamed a guard's voice, "must jump over one of the
> pits and land on the other side. Those who miss will get what they
> rightfully deserve—ra-ta-ta-ta-ta."
>
> In the darkness, unable to make out the width of the pits, the
> prisoners nonetheless knew that even a young man in daylight at
> his most energetic would have been unable to jump them.
>
> Among the thousands who stood in the field that night was the
> rabbi of Bluzhov, Rabbi Israel Spira, along with a close friend and
> follower. The friend, who didn't want to "entertain" the Germans
> by even *attempting* to jump the pit tried to persuade the rebbe to
> simply sit down and wait for the bullets that would end their
> "wretched existence."
>
> As they drew near the pit, the rabbi "glanced down at his feet,
> the swollen feet of a fifty-three-year-old Jew ridden with starva-
> tion and disease," then he looked at his friend, a "skeleton with
> burning eyes." Gripping his friend's hand, he suddenly exclaimed:
> "We are jumping!"

With that, they closed their eyes—and when they opened them, they were standing on the other side of the pit! As the younger man stood weeping, he turned to the rabbi. "Spira, for your sake, I am alive; indeed, there must be a God in heaven. Tell me, Rebbe, how did you do it?"

"I was holding on to my ancestral merit," the rebbe replied. "I was holding on to the coattails of my father, and my grandfather and my great-grandfather, of blessed memory."

The rebbe, however, was curious about one thing. "Tell me, my friend," he said, "how did *you* reach the other side of the pit?"

"I was holding on to you," replied the rabbi's friend.[10]

What a lovely story! And what a great illustration of the deep confidence that the Hasidim have for their holy leaders. Since Hasidism's inception, rebbes have instilled awe in the hearts of their followers, and modern Hasidim are no exception. In *The Midrash Says,* a modern mystical commentary on the Torah, tzaddikim (not all tzaddikim are rebbes, but all rebbes are tzaddikim) are believed to be divided into seven groups: those that (1) radiate like the sun, (2) shine like the moon, (3) sparkle like the sky, (4) gleam like stars, (5) flash like lightning, (6) radiate beauty like roses, and (7) glimmer like the golden menorah of the Bais Hamikdash (Temple).[11]

Even if an occasional rebbe's legend *isn't* accompanied by flamboyant tales, he remains a holy figure who stands above all those around him. One of the Breslover rebbe's closest followers and biographers, for instance, was said to have had an aversion to tales of the miraculous, undoubtedly because the rebbe himself believed that each person, not just a select few, could attain the highest level of spirituality. Oddly enough, however, this is supposed to be the only Hasidic sect whose original rebbe, Nachman of Breslov, had no successor because, in the words of one writer, no one could fill his shoes.

Hasidim try to regularly visit the graves of their rebbes. Doing this can, at minimum, inspire one with a new zest for spirituality, but most pious Hasidim take this much further. Being at a rebbe's grave is a mystical experience: prayers are answered, healings occur, and lives are changed.

A mystical regard for the dead certainly isn't confined to the Hasidim. In Catholicism, saints' bodies are preserved and thought to retain mystical powers affecting those who visit their tombs. Indeed, Catholic leaders have often been hard-pressed to keep deceased saints from being torn apart. St. Teresa of Avila is said to have reached her final resting place without her left arm, right foot, some fingers from her right hand, some ribs, most of her neck, part of her jaw, her left eye, and her heart. Generalissimo Franco kept her left hand by his bedside until he died.[12]

Most people, however, respect the body and dispose of it in some ritualistic manner. Some regard the burial or crematory site as sacred. Native American burial grounds, for instance, are among their most sacred lands.

Recently, I had lunch with a friend from my church. Samira is from the town of Shiraz, Iran, where one of the greatest Sufi[13] saints ever, Hafiz, was born and is buried. Having grown up in a Sufi family, Samira remembers visiting Hafiz's grave and watching as young couples prayed there, reading poetry and hoping that Hafiz's saintly power would enable them to conceive.

The examples are endless, but it's important to know that the Hasidim are far from unique in their regard for the graves of holy saints.

A visit to the grave of a rebbe is something I haven't had the privilege of experiencing personally, but I did have the opportunity to watch a video of another person's experience, and I've also listened to stories of several male friends who had traveled to New

York on a rebbe's *yahrzeit*—the date of his death, on which souls are said to receive a special spiritual elevation—for the sole purpose of visiting his grave.

The seventh and latest Lubavitcher rebbe, Menachem Mendel Schneerson, passed away in 1994, childless, after forty-four years of leading Chabad and endowing it with its greatest strength; Chabad leaders then agreed that he would be their last rebbe. Some Lubavitchers believe he was the Messiah and that he'll rise from the dead, but most believe only that he was a tzaddik—a very holy man with great spiritual powers that continue to be unleashed even in his death. One of my friends, who isn't Hasidic, had such a profound experience when he visited the rebbe's grave that, even though he stops short of calling him the Messiah, he also hesitates to emphatically deny it.

On special days, many thousands may flock to the rebbe's grave. On the video that Rabbi G. loaned me, twenty-five thousand men and women lined the sidewalks and paths, waiting to pray at the rebbe's grave and to absorb the holiness of the rooms where he studied and rested. Men and women are ushered through his private quarters in segregated groups, but only men are allowed inside his study.

Thousands of letters are left at the grave, and rabbis instruct people to write anything they want, whatever's on their minds or in their hearts. Have no negative thoughts, though, the rabbis sometimes say, because this is one of the holiest places in the entire universe. Women burst into tears of joy, and men, overcome by emotion, are sometimes unable to speak.

My own friend said that the rebbe's grave wasn't at all like a grave. "It was a happy place," he said, finally able to speak of it for the first time many months after he'd returned to Dallas. "It was like the rebbe was alive and was communicating with us."

"Potent spiritual energies" are said to permeate a tzaddik's grave, and thus a rebbe never loses his ability to change the life of his followers. He remains, in death, larger than life.

One night, after a late study at Rabbi G.'s home, a young man walked with me to my car and we stood in the road talking for nearly an hour. Because I had just returned the video of the rebbe's grave, David wanted to know if I had had any spiritual experiences when I watched it. "Yes," I said, "I felt aware of a deep connection between this world and the next."

"I wondered if you might say something like that," David said quietly. "That feeling is the essence of Chassidus."

As I drove home, David's words reverberated over and over in my mind. How I loved their mysticism and their incredible comfort with realms and experiences that lay outside the West's excessive rationalism. The more I was around the Hasidim, the more I found myself becoming intimately involved with the world of spirit and mystery.

It's estimated that about two hundred different Hasidic sects exist today, though that's counting small, mostly localized groups. Many groups were wiped out during the Shoah, or Holocaust.[14]

Moment magazine describes one of these groups, the Lubavitchers, as an international presence, with more than thirty-seven hundred couples conducting "missionary" work (again, the Lubavitchers are interested in helping *Jews* become more observant, not in converting people from other faiths) in more than one hundred countries. Nearly fifty thousand additional professional workers assist them. Lubavitcher institutions number about twenty-six hundred worldwide.[15]

One sizeable Hasidic group in Israel is the Breslover sect. The Breslovers[16] are known as the "dead Hasidim" because they're the only ones to have had just one rebbe, Nachman of Breslov (1772–1810).

Surprisingly, Rabbi Nachman himself left a historical legacy, described by Arthur Green in *Tormented Master,* as a rabbi who was an ascetic, associated suffering with holiness, and was subject to "rapid mood swings." Nachman, nonetheless, was (and is) a much-loved master, inspiring a great movement based, in part, on the belief that all could (and can) achieve his level of spirituality.[17] In addition, one modern Hasid points out that the Breslovers are characterized, as are all Hasidim, by an emphasis on the heart in the service of God and by living life with joy and intensity.

My opportunity to study with a Breslover rabbi came during my Torah retreat to Colorado. Rabbi Natan was one of the most gregarious men I've ever met, utterly charismatic, with a warmth and exuberance that immediately drew me in. Young and handsome, with a wild, graying beard, he had founded a Breslover yeshiva in Jerusalem, which he currently heads. Although his teaching was deep and thoughtful, he could have told about painting a room in his house and I would have been captivated.

Rabbi Natan taught us, as all good Jewish teachers do, that the questions are the most important part of the study. During his sessions, he'd prod us to come up with dozens and dozens of questions, then, still not satisfied, he'd choose a question and ask us how many questions the question itself raised. "Anyone can come up with answers," he'd say, "but it's the questions that matter."

"Look at the rhythm of the passage," Rabbi Natan instructed us. By doing this, we'd learn how to *feel* what we read, looking at it intuitively before we dug in analytically. He reminded us that every stage of our journey was important and that we should never think merely of the destination. And then he'd plunge into mysticism, encouraging us to bring divine energy into the world and then, having released it, to work with it. "If you're moving," he said, "then the world around you is moving."

Rabbi Natan taught with wildly waving hands and told one story after another. Once he forgot the ending to one of them and, blushing red as a ripe strawberry, appealed to the other rabbis and guest teachers. Everyone had heard the story, but all had heard different endings. After all the endings had been given, Rabbi Natan made up still another one and told us to take our choice.

Another rabbi teaching that week was a shy Vizhnitzer named Rabbi Akiva, who often stood in a corner by himself when our study groups took breaks, gathering in noisy groups to talk and grab a snack.

Each day Rabbi Akiva taught several classes. The retreat was designed so that we alternated studying in small groups, then paired off with a *chevruta* in order to discuss and debate what we'd just learned. Usually, Rabbi Akiva spoke so softly that even if I sat only two or three chairs away from him, I'd have to strain to hear. However, when he'd come to something that excited him, his voice would rise so quickly and dramatically that the other study groups, scattered across the large room, would swing around to see what was going on.

One morning, Rabbi Akiva was discussing a scripture passage in which a man was ordered to be put to death by Moses for openly fornicating with a Midianite woman. A young man in our group questioned this: "How could Israel have the death penalty for a sexual relationship with a non-Jew?" he wondered out loud.

Rabbi Akiva had a number of answers, which he stated in his softest voice. Obviously, Moses didn't have the man put to death for having sex with a Midianite woman, the rabbi said; Moses himself was married to a Midianite. The passage instead indicates that in some way, by his actions, this man was inciting Israel to open rebellion, and he was affecting a good many people. Further, Rabbi Akiva said, the man was a prince and there seemed to be an indication that he was actually having sex with the woman in full public view.

For a few moments the rabbi sat quietly, his sharp eyes boring through each of us. Then suddenly, leaping halfway to his feet, the rabbi reminded the young man—loudly—of how rare it was for anyone to actually receive the death penalty in Israel. The verdict had to be unanimous, with the entire seventy men of the Sanhedrin, Rabbi Akiva stated to the entire room, who were now all listening, and there had to be two witnesses to the actual crime, he said, pounding the table, and when they did sentence someone to death, all had to resign and they would forever after be known as a bloody court. Then Rabbi Akiva sat back down and calmly resumed his teaching, with all of us straining to hear him.

Rabbi Akiva taught of the miracles God performed in Israel— vastly more spectacular than any I'd read in scripture. When the Temple sacrifice was made, he said, the smoke would rise straight into the heavens. Even if there was a wind, it would rise straight up. Nothing could pollute the Beit Midrash; there were not even any flies in it.

The rabbi taught us the meaning of Hasidic practices. When they dry their hands after ritual washing, he said, they raise the right one a little higher to symbolize that kindness is greater than strength, the right hand symbolizing kindness and the left, strength. A Hasid's clothing buttons like that of a woman's, he told us, again, right over left, for the same symbolic purpose.

He told us about his rebbe and how he frequently told jokes that no one understood but that they'd laugh loudly out of respect.

At the end of each class, everyone would shout, *"Yasher koach,"* ("May your strength be firm"), and Rabbi Akiva would beam, asking us if we had "learned and received anything of value" from the class. "I just want you to take away something important," he'd say after each lesson. "I just want you to take something away with you." We always did.

Because Rabbi Akiva, when he wasn't teaching, almost always stood quietly by himself, I was hesitant to approach and talk to him. But finally, my curiosity overcame my courtesy and I struck up a conversation. He told me proudly that he had ten children, all of them either Lubavitchers or married to one, and his parents and siblings were all Lubavitcher. Having chosen to follow the Vizhnitzer rebbe made him the black sheep of the family.

When he told me he was from Canada, I launched into a story of a visit I'd made to Canada in which, during each and every bus ride to town, some thoroughly drunk man would make a ruckus and the bus driver would threaten to kick him off the bus. Then one day, I told the rabbi, we passed a store called a "loonie store" (a Canadian money exchange), and I looked at my husband and said, "Voila! That's where they get these people!"

Rabbi Akiva threw his head back and his laughter filled the room. Eyes sparkling, he made crazy circles around his ears and laughed again. After this, I sat with him once or twice during meals or approached him to talk, and I always received a warm and hearty reception, along with eager conversation.

On the second day of the retreat, during a break, I had wandered outside to take a short walk when Rabbi Natan's wife caught up with me. Because I was the only non-Jew present, the story of my spiritual journey and my interest in Judaism had already circulated among virtually everyone present. Ruth (Rabbi Natan's wife) pried me quietly with questions, then told me that this was her first trip with her husband in which she hadn't brought any of her ten children.

"Who's keeping your children this trip?" I asked.

"My children," she smiled. "The oldest is sixteen and she's watching the younger ones."

After a while, we returned to the group, where the study had already resumed. I thought of how odd we must have looked walking together, me in my blue jeans with pink-painted toenails sticking out of my clogs, Ruth in her long Israeli dress, her head completely covered by a *sheitel*. Nonetheless, we became fast friends and spent many of our breaks walking and talking.

The morning I left, Ruth hurried to catch me and slipped me her address. "If you ever come to Jerusalem, please call me. I'd love to show you around, show you the yeshiva, our home, our city."

I scratched my address on a piece of paper also and handed it to her; a couple of weeks after I arrived home, I received a letter from her with pictures of the sloping landscape outside her home and several of her children rolling down a hill, their mouths poised in screams of laughter as they played with one another.

I wrote her back and included an unbreakable jar of jalapenos, reminding her of a humorous incident that happened one night at dinner. That night, I had sat across from Ruth and Rabbi Natan and had apparently dumped too much horseradish on my plate, causing a startled Ruth to warn me about how hot horseradish is. "I'm from Texas," I had grinned at her. "I eat jalapenos." Rabbi Natan had laughed uproariously, asking his wife if she knew what a jalapeno was. "No," she said, shyly. So back home, I had sent her a jar of them, hoping they were kosher.

The Hasidim, as I've said, are the mystical sect of Judaism and regard kabbalistic books as sacred texts that illuminate the deeper meaning of Torah. Hasidim believe that one should only begin study of kabbalah at the age of forty, after one has some mastery of Torah and Talmud and is at a mature enough age to delve into the deeper mysteries. One writer points out that it was believed that delving into kabbalah before the age of forty could result in insanity.[18]

Because these books are sacred to the Hasidim, they despise superficial tampering with them. After the pop star Madonna announced some years back that she was studying kabbalah, it became a standing joke with Rabbi G. and our little study group. "Ask Madonna," he'd say when someone would ask a question. "She knows kabbalah."

Rabbi Alan Lew, known as the "zen rabbi" because of his interest in bringing certain principles of Zen Buddhism into his observance of Judaism, writes of his experience studying kabbalah with a great master of the mystical text. As he studied, Rabbi Lew noted that the world became nothing to him, that he actually began to live in the world of forms described by kabbalistic texts. Others in his group became so absorbed that they gave up jobs as teachers and research scientists, pulled by the "mysterious magnetism" of kabbalah.

During this time, Lew began to understand why serious mystics expected a student of kabbalah to be mature and thoroughly familiar with Torah and Talmud. "I had studied Talmud for six years at JTS [Jewish Theological Seminary]," writes Lew, "and I was one of the best Talmud students there . . . but Kabbalah presented another degree of difficulty altogether."

When Lew finally returned to the "real world," he remembered his mystical immersion as "one of the most intense spiritual places [he] had ever inhabited." For the rest of his life, he would know what kabbalah was and wasn't and would reject the "charlatans teaching nonsense in the name of Kabbalah."[19]

One of the most fascinating aspects of Jewish mysticism to me has been the idea that the Hebrew language holds special mystical powers and was, indeed, the means of creation. The Tanya tells us that the twenty-two letters of the Hebrew alphabet (which are not merely letters but "distinct forms of Divine manifestation") are "able to create a vast multitude of creatures." If the letters are combined in one way, a certain kind of creature is formed; combine the letters in a different manner, and a new creature comes into being.

Even the way individual letters of the Hebrew alphabet are shaped has significance. According to one Lubavitcher commentary, the shape of the letters "indicates the pattern of the flow and manifestation of the light and life-force and power which is revealed and flows through this letter."[20]

God's most holy name, YHVH, says one writer, consists of three Hebrew letters, *yud, heh,* and *vav. Yud,* a "simple point," indicates a state of "concealment and obscurity," whereas the letter *heh*'s extension in length and breadth points to a "flow . . . into concealed worlds." *Vav,* which is shaped like a vertical line, is the attribute of God that flows downward into the world.[21]

I can't get enough of the stories related to the mystical properties of the Hebrew language. One evening, Rabbi G. was teaching from the Torah about the giving of the commandments on Mount Sinai to Moses and, in answer to one of his questions, I mentioned that Moses had broken the first set of tablets in anger after he came down from the mountain and saw that the Israelites had, in their doubt and impatience, constructed a golden calf to worship.

"Ah," said Rabbi G., "that is not how we believe. The stones would have been far too heavy for Moshe [Moses] to carry, but the Hebrew letters made them light. When Moshe came down from the mountain and saw the idol, the holy letters floated away and the stones became their normal weight. So Moshe could no longer carry them. He dropped them and they broke."

I better understood this way of thinking when I thought of the Hebrew language as sound. This, more than an actual written language, has parallels in many other religions. Christianity, for instance, teaches that Jesus, as the Word, participated in creation. Certain Sufi orders believe that the universe was created and is sustained by certain sounds. In Hindu thought, the perfect sound of "om" is thought to bring us into a more perfect spiritual state, helping us to better attune to the Being of God.

Rabbi Alan Lew explains that the *Shema,* the most revered prayer in Judaism, consists of three primary sounds. The Hebrew letter *sheen* (or shin), pronounced "shh" is, he writes, the "sound of cacophony." The letter *mem* is the harmony of all sound (same as "om" for Hindus). The letter *ayin* is the "silence that contains all sound."[22]

In the Hebrew and Greek Testaments, numbers always have a symbolic meaning, and understanding this has made the Bible, for me, far richer.

For mystical Jews, the precise number of Hebrew words (as well as their arrangement) refers to different manifestations of God. In addition (no pun intended), simple numbers signify divine things; groups of ten, celestial beings and objects; multiples of hundreds, the terrestrial world; and thousands branch into the afterlife.[23]

One interesting and recurring theme in Hasidic and mystical thought is the idea of seven levels, or worlds, from which God was driven by sinful humans, then brought back by righteous ones. When Adam sinned, God moved to the second world. Enoch pushed God to the second and then was driven further and further by the generation of which Noah was a part, then by the builders of the Tower of Babel, the Egyptians and the Sodomites; finally, the Egyptians pushed God to the outermost and highest firmament. Seven righteous individuals, however, brought God back, beginning with Abraham and culminating with Moses.

A few years ago, Hesha asked me to work part of a day at Ruach Torah's booth at the annual Jewish Arts Fest in Dallas—a festival that takes place in Dallas's beautiful Meyerson Symphony Hall. It's one of our local Jewish community's largest events.

Ruach Torah's booth was number 39, which Hesha had requested. Why? One-third of this number (13) is the numerical equivalent for *ahav,* love in Hebrew, and we're to love God with the entirety of the three parts of our being: our heart, soul, and mind. Hence, 3 times 13 is 39; the number of our booth was "triple-strength" love.

People often ask me whether I believe all of this, but those who ask simply don't understand mysticism, for mysticism is something we don't apprehend with the intellect. It's irrelevant whether we "believe" it or not. What's important is that we remain open to its mysterious effects on our lives and being and that we gain a comfort being in the realm of the unknown and, to some degree, that of the unknowable.

In Nikos Kazantzakis's famous novel, *Zorba the Greek,* the narrator, Zorba's closest companion, tells of a moment when he began to understand what intuitive living meant. "Awakening in me was the soul of the first men on earth, such as it was before it became totally detached from the universe, when it still felt the truth directly, without the distorting influence of reason," he reflects.[24]

Knowledge in Chassidus, teaches Rabbi G., means limitation. Adam and Eve were above knowledge, he says, and eating from the tree brought them down. I used to wonder, when I read this story, how knowledge could possibly be considered a bad thing. Jewish mysticism, however, offers me an explanation. A direct experience of God lies above the intellect, above knowledge, and if we desire to unite with God, to have a direct experience of God, we must rise above it.

Such teaching goes against all I, a Westerner, had previously embraced. Yet my forays into the world of mystery began to permeate my heart and mind. I began to understand that experience of God lies beyond the world of books and teachers. The mystics in Judaism have taught me that when I leave the world of *assiyah,* the physical world, I leave behind questions of whether something is literally true. I enter the world of *atzilut*—the world where I intuit and experience union with God, the world where the questions of the intellect are no longer of any importance.

One evening during my studies with Rabbi G., a discussion came up concerning the meaning of a certain story in Torah. Rabbi G. gave a Hasidic interpretation, but a knowledgeable student, one who was moving toward becoming a Hasid himself, disputed this. "I've been taught a different interpretation," he argued.

Rabbi G. replied that he wasn't saying anyone was wrong but that he "just wanted to take [us] deeper."

"Well, this is what I've been taught," said Moshe.

Back and forth they went, citing texts and rabbis and logic, until Rabbi G. finally gave up. "OK, OK!" he said, shrugging his shoulders and rolling his eyes toward the ceiling. "You're right! You're right! I'm only trying to take you deeper."

Then, plunging back into the mysteries in which he lived each day, Rabbi G. began to take us deeper.

CHAPTER SEVEN

Hungering for My Roots

I t's a spring evening in Dallas, Texas, and I'm at a beautiful downtown cathedral—the mother church of the Roman Catholic diocese, which includes nine counties and more than fifty thousand registered households. Built during the early part of the century and now a startling presence in Dallas's arts district, the cathedral opens its doors each weekend to offer mass to around eleven thousand people.

Tonight, however, the most central and prominent section of seats, which extends from the front of the cathedral to the back, is reserved for and quickly filling up with Jews, many of whom seem to feel more at ease here than I do. I cross the aisle to talk with some friends from Temple Emanu-El, who ask me if I've ever been to this cathedral. No, I tell them. In fact, other than some churches I saw on tours of Mexico, I've only been inside a Catholic church once in my life. My Jewish friends describe what the cathedral looked like before its recent renovations. I'm amazed when they tell me they've been here several times for interfaith services.

During this particular service, a permanent menorah will be installed at the front of the sanctuary. Before the service begins, I join several people on the podium as we gaze at the menorah. Seven black, elongated figures, El Greco style, hold the candlesticks. One is the figure of a rabbi; the others represent the six million Jews who were killed during the Shoah. The menorah, created by Israeli sculptor Aharon Bezalel, is a replica of the Yom Hashoah (Holocaust Remembrance Day) menorah presented to Pope John Paul II in 1999.

As I return to my seat, I pass a rabbi who's making her way to the podium. Several Catholics call to her, "Hello, Rabbi!" And they whisper to those around them that she's one of the rabbis from Temple Emanu-El.

I pick up my program, which reads:

Forgiveness and Reconciliation
MENORAH DEDICATION
Cathedral Santuario de Guadalupe
Dallas, Texas
May 22, 2002

Soon the service begins, and Rudy Baum, who lost his parents in the Shoah, speaks first. He brings home for us the number "six million." More Jews were killed, he says, than all the Jews living in the United States today. More Jews were killed than all the Jews who live in Israel. Turning to Bishop Grahmann, who was seated on the podium, he thanks him for accepting the menorah and for asking that it be placed in the "mother church." John Paul II, Mr. Baum tells us, has done more than anyone in history to bring about reconciliation. He is grateful.

Rabbis and reverends take turns speaking to the congregation. A cellist plays *Kol Nidre,* composed by a man who converted to Christianity in his youth and returned to his own faith thirty-five years later; not many years afterward, in 1939, he gave the Jews a melody that all know and love even today. Each of the menorah's candles are then lit, one by one, by Jewish and Christian leaders.

As I sat there, I silently gave thanks for the progress we've made in loving and understanding one another. Interfaith groups are springing up everywhere. Churches and synagogues share services, meals, and conversation. Christians are laying aside their long-held belief in their exclusive status with God.[1] Jews are laying aside their pain and distrust. We are coming together.

Diana L. Eck, a scholar, writer, and Christian whose outlook was transformed after studying in India and immersing herself in the spirituality of the Hindu religion, writes that in modern America, Christians, Jews, Hindus, Buddhists, and Muslims are virtually next-door neighbors. Yet what is new today, she writes, isn't the diversity of religious traditions but rather our "sharply heightened *awareness*" [emphasis mine] of this diversity throughout the world and the fact that we feel an increasing need to understand people and faiths other than our own.[2]

In her book *Life on the Fringes,* Haviva Ner-David, an Orthodox Jew, struggles with memories of her parents' reluctance to wear certain highly visible signs of their Judaism when she was growing up. "Multiculturalism did not exist then," she writes, "and differences were frowned upon, even discriminated against." Today, however, at least to some extent, cultural and religious differences are celebrated. "Looking and acting like a Jew is no longer a source of shame."[3]

As I write these words, I'm thinking about a dinner I attended a short time ago. I had sat beside a Hindu and across from a Jew who sat in between a Sikh and a Buddhist. There were Sufis present, as well as a Wiccan priest, a Baha'i, and a Muslim. There were whites, blacks, Indians, and Asians, and those of Middle Eastern descent. No one had assigned seats for us; we just, in everything that seems contrary to human nature, gravitated to others who looked different from us.

This amazes me and causes me to ask, Where have we been and where are we going with our increasing interest in one another? And, with Jews and Christians, what are our differences and what draws us together in a common spirituality and worship? What I've discovered in the hundreds of Jewish services, studies, and events I've attended has answered some of these questions.

The hunger of Christians to learn about the Jewish faith is astounding. Most of this stems from our fairly recent realization that the roots of the Christian faith are thoroughly Jewish. We grew up knowing Jesus was a Jew and that the Bible was written almost in its entirety by Jews, but somehow we're only just now *grasping* this fact. Embarrassing, but true.

Several years ago, I heard Howard Cohen, a dentist, speak at the Jewish Arts Fest in Dallas. The so-called New Testament, he said, states that Christians were "grafted in"—that Christians were supposed to be new branches, not a new tree. He didn't agree with the literalism with which many Christians approach the Bible, he added, since, from a Jewish perspective, the Bible is designed to evoke images and spiritual lessons, which are made clearer by commentaries called midrash.

When Howard mentioned that he often spoke in churches, I approached him to see if he'd speak at ours, but he was booked a year in advance—in churches! Virtually every single Sunday morning, "Howard the Jew," as he calls himself, stands in front of some Sunday school class in the Dallas area teaching the Greek

Testament in ways that few Christians get to hear. If he, a Jew, had walked in the time of Jesus, how would he have heard his stories? What would he, a Jew, have thought of Jesus? These are the types of questions he addresses.

Christians want to know the answers. We're clamoring to listen to him, to gain a deeper understanding of the Bible, and to regain some of our Jewish roots.

After I told my Sunday school class about Howard, we booked him for a month—the amount of time he usually spends at any one church—more than a year in advance. When he finally arrived, we grabbed him for another month, another year in advance. When that month arrived, and he told us he'd had a cancellation for the following month, we asked him to stay, bumping other teachers, extending his teaching for a sixth week, then a seventh.

Howard effortlessly keeps his audiences spellbound. During his first Sunday with us, Howard bounces into the room and asks where we want to start. When someone asks a question, he spends nearly an hour answering it—sort of. Actually, he veers off on dozens of tangents, sometimes asking us to remind him what the question was. "I'm getting around to your question," he says five or six times; eventually, he does.

Howard attends an Orthodox synagogue, though he doesn't hold to the high level of ritual observance that most other members there hold to. But have no doubt about it—Howard is a Jew. Not a Messianic one. Just a Jew. He's knowledgeable, charismatic, frank, and funny. "This is what that story meant before you people got hold of it," he grins, launching into what is, for us, a revolutionary interpretation of something Jesus did or said. "My car wasn't vandalized," he says, "so I guess you're OK with everything I said last week." When the Jews think that the Christians have finally "got him," he says, he just throws in a little jab at Christianity, then they relax and he can come back, without alarming anyone, and teach in Sunday school classes for another couple of months.

Howard also delights in talking to Jews, throwing around quotes from famous and respected rabbis, and tossing in something Jesus said. When he tells the group it's a quote from Jesus, Howard says, at least three Jews always pass out. "Jesus was an observant Jew," he tells them.

Why does Howard spend so much time teaching in churches? He respects Christians, he says. His wife was one when they met. He believes it's a good deed to bridge differences between people. Christians will gain a greater understanding of and respect for Judaism and for Jews, and as a result, Jews will feel more comfortable and accepted for who they are.

Howard gleans some of his information from a scholar named Geza Vermes, who has written a trilogy of books on Jesus from a Jewish perspective. Vermes is a Jewish scholar who's an expert on the Greek Testament and who writes on the subject to a popular audience.

At the age of six, Vermes, along with his parents (who were Hungarian Jews), converted to Christianity; when Vermes was eighteen, he decided to enter the priesthood. Although the church hid him during the Shoah, in which both of his parents died, he searched in vain for a Catholic order that would admit him, finally finding a home with the Notre-Dame de Sion, an order for which one original aim had been to convert Jews. Nice fit.

However, "eventually, gradually, unceremoniously," writes Magen Broshi in a book review, [Vermes] "reconverted" and joined the Liberal Synagogue in London, where he had been living, teaching, and doing research work. "Some people apparently do not know that Christianity was not the religion of Jesus," writes Broshi, "but very few people know what the religion of Jesus really was."[4]

To help correct this, he says, Vermes devoted many years of research, resulting in three books about Jesus the Jew.

In Vermes's view, Jesus followed Jewish law, attended synagogue, and communicated in a Jewish manner. Many of the gospel passages in which Jesus is said to have undermined the law, Vermes believes, have been misinterpreted. Vermes shows that most of Jesus' actions, stories, and teachings were in line with the teaching of the Jews of his day.

For instance, Jesus is often seen as denigrating the Sabbath law of refraining from work because he defended his disciples for picking grain and eating it on the Sabbath. However, when Jesus replied to those who criticized him for this action, he backed up his actions with a story from the Hebrew scriptures in which King David had set an acceptable precedent, entering the "house of God," along with his "companions," and eating the consecrated bread that only priests were allowed to eat. Far from flippantly disregarding the rules of the Sabbath, Jesus had a great regard for them and sidestepped them only when there seemed to be biblical authority for doing so.[5]

"Nowhere in the Gospels is Jesus depicted as deliberately setting out to deny or substantially alter any commandment of the Torah in itself," writes Vermes. "The controversial statements turn either on conflicting laws where one has to override the other, or on the precise understanding of the full extent of a precept."[6] In other words, Jesus was illuminating Torah, just as other Jewish leaders did, not disputing it.

Another prolific writer who addresses a popular audience and depicts Jesus from a Jewish perspective is the distinguished professor and rabbi Jacob Neusner. Neusner, however, comes to an entirely different conclusion than does Vermes. Jesus, he says, came into conflict with Jewish law at every turn and, were Neusner to have lived in his day and heard him speak, he would have concluded that he, as a Jew, would have been unable to follow him.

On the issue of picking grain on the Sabbath, Neusner quotes Jesus as saying, "It is lawful to do good on the Sabbath." The Sabbath, however, writes Neusner, isn't about doing good; it's about holiness. Jesus' statement, he writes, is entirely beside the point.[7]

Neusner tells us in his preface that he studies and writes about Jesus because of his respect for his many Christian friends. He wants to engage us in dialogue.

Groups that help Christians and Jews are springing up everywhere. It seems everyone I meet tells me that their church or synagogue has an active interfaith group. Just yesterday in church, I sat beside a couple of guests who told me that their Baptist church regularly plans services with a Conservative synagogue in their area, which was a surprise to me because I had the impression that only the Reform movement in Judaism was interested in formal interfaith relationships.

One interfaith dialogue group began in 1986 as a graduate seminar conducted by a Christian professor and a rabbi. The response was encouraging enough to conduct a second seminar, for which 137 signed up. Soon the men began receiving requests to present their seminar at local churches, then invitations poured in from other cities, churches, and universities, ultimately resulting in a book. Such a response is another indication of the high level of interest that Jews and Christians have in getting to know each other and understanding each other's faiths.

The authors believe that as we've begun to dialogue with each other, we're realizing how much we have in common and that we can walk the path to God together, even if our ways diverge at some points.[8]

For me, setting about to learn about the origins of my own faith plunged me into a love affair with Judaism. It became a deeply fulfilling path for me, in addition to the paths I already follow, to experience God more richly and in a broader manner. From the beginning, I loved Jewish rituals, the Jews' passion for God, their spirituality, and the sweeping way they engaged their texts.

The deepest enrichment comes, I believe, not when we merely talk with one another but when we enter into the other's faith experience. God is such a vast and unfathomable Being, how can I think that my own faith knows all there is to know or that we have the only word on who God is and how he should be worshiped?

At a recent interfaith dinner I attended, Judie Arkow, who founded the group, asked each of us to say why we were there and what we wanted to gain from our experience. All the participants shared their views, mostly that they wanted to get to know people of other faiths and, by doing so, help create a more peaceful and tolerant community.

I felt that way also, but I felt more. So when it came my turn to speak, I told the group that although I wanted to get to know them, I also wanted to know and experience their God. For me, dialogue isn't enough. I want to find new ways to worship and experience God.

As I've studied and worshiped with the Jews, I've come to understand both the beliefs and attitudes that unite us and those that separate. It has seemed to me that one of the biggest obstacles for the Jews in their relationship with Christians is the belief among many Christians that they have an exclusive relationship with God and the resulting effort to convert Jews.

Christian belief in exclusivity is changing, although it's still a predominant belief among evangelicals. Bailey Smith's infamous statement that God doesn't hear the prayer of Jews was a reflection of his belief that because of the Jewish rejection of Jesus as Messiah, God has turned his back on the Jews and embraced the Christians. "You all have probably forgotten that statement," Howard Cohen recently said to my Sunday school class, "but we haven't." The pain that statements such as these cause Jews is heart-wrenching.

The groups that particularly annoy my Jewish friends are the Messianic congregations, consisting of lifelong Christians and of Jews who have converted to Christianity and take it as their special mission to convince Jews to accept Jesus as their Messiah.

My personal experience with Messianic congregants hasn't been positive. A couple of years ago, for instance, I was given the name of a man from whom I could buy rare Jewish texts. As we talked, I was astounded to learn that he was as interested in Judaism as I was, yet still considered himself a Christian. He was not only very well informed about Judaism but he loved to attend synagogue and Jewish holiday services.

"Are you involved with a Messianic congregation?" I asked, a little suspicious.

"Absolutely not!" he said.

I pressed him further. "Are you involved with Judaism for its own sake or because you want to learn ways to reach Jews for Jesus?"

"I just love Judaism!" he said, without hesitation. "No ulterior motives."

Several days later, the books arrived that I had ordered from this man, and inside one book was an enclosure that read, "My name is Brian Alderman [name changed] and I live in Nebraska. My heart and ministry is to see the people of G-d brought back to their first love. To encourage them to be excited about their G-d and give hope and strength that G-d is still in love with them! And with this excitement we might see more unbelievers come to know Yeshua as their Messiah!"

I was, and still am, flabbergasted.

The terminology many Messianic congregations use imitates that of Judaism, and they often design their churches to look like synagogues. Unsuspecting Jews, usually from other countries, may attend without ever realizing they're entering a church.

This was brought home to me one day when I was on my way to my friend Reid's home in North Dallas. Having passed what I took to be a synagogue, I asked Reid if he'd ever attended the synagogue in his neighborhood.

"What synagogue?" he asked, genuinely bewildered. Then, realizing what I was talking about, he groaned. "That isn't a synagogue," he sighed. "It's a Messianic congregation. They built that one and two others in the center of the Jewish community so they could proselytize."

Another evening, Rabbi G. explained that Russian Jews, because they often arrive in this country knowing nothing about their own faith, are among the most susceptible to being fooled by Messianic congregations. "The only way they know they're Jews," he explained, "is because it's on their identification cards." When Messianic members knock on their door, inviting them to "synagogue," they often have no idea they're being invited to a church.

Members of Messianic congregations sometimes disrupt Jewish events. At the Jewish Arts Fest last year, for instance, during a question-and-answer period with Howard Cohen, one Messianic congregant attempted to dominate the entire session, asking question after question, each designed to put a Jew on the spot, back him into a corner, and force him to think about whether Jesus is the Messiah.

One of the problems I have with these congregations is that Christians who attend there aren't getting an authentic knowledge of Judaism. They receive virtually all their information from Christians and from converted Jews, some of whom weren't raised in an observant home.

Most Jews I know don't have a problem with these congregations incorporating Jewish elements into their services. They merely ask that they call themselves Christians—a truthful label that separates their churches from synagogues and their ministers from rabbis. They merely ask that they stop using subtle methods to represent themselves and to acquire Jewish converts.

Another hindrance that I've noticed in Jewish-Christian relationships is a misunderstanding of certain Jewish practices and beliefs. One of these has to do with the refusal by many rabbis to perform interfaith marriages.

Not all Jews, of course, are against intermarriage, though religious Jews, for the most part, are. Still, according to one report, more than half of the world's thirteen to fourteen million Jews are marrying people of other faiths.[9] Some say the trend toward intermarriage won't change, and it angers them when Jewish institutions and synagogues refuse to sanction these marriages.

A couple of years ago, during an Internet discussion on the topic, the dean of admissions at the Academy for Jewish Religion stated that people who have a non-Jewish partner are ineligible for admission to the academy, and if they acquire such a partner during their studies, they're ineligible for ordination.[10]

The response? One woman wrote and said that such a policy encourages intermarried Jews to move away from the Jewish community rather than toward it. Another wrote, "What a shame if the Jewish community loses the great potential you have to offer as a rabbi because somebody does not approve of whom you fell in love with!" Still another pointed out that she had family members raised by two Jewish parents who had abandoned their faith and others raised by only one Jewish parent who were vibrant, religious Jewish adults. Others, of course, disagreed, believing it's a reasonable requirement for rabbis and cantors to be married to those of their own faith.

But what about laypeople and the refusal of many rabbis, including about two-thirds of Reform rabbis in the United States and nearly all in the United Kingdom and Canada, to perform intermarriages?[11] The primary concern seems to be for the children, though the partnership itself, many believe, is strengthened when marrying within one's own faith.

Because Jews continue to marry outside their own faith, however, Reform and other movements have made concessions so as not to alienate those who want to continue to practice their faith. Whereas in the Orthodox faith, a child must have a Jewish mother (the father determines what tribe the child is part of) in order to be considered Jewish, Reform considers a child Jewish if he's raised Jewish, regardless of whether his mother or father is Jewish.

Non-Jewish spouses in the more liberal movements of Judaism are encouraged to be part of the life of the synagogue, and often they agree to sign a statement that they'll raise their children in the Jewish faith. This seems rankling on the surface, even to me, but it has to be understood that the Jews in America are a minority, and their religion is weakened, in quantity and in its inner strength, as Jews intermarry and are assimilated into the dominant secular or Christian culture.

This issue has arisen in my own family. Fifteen years ago, my nephew Glen, then working on his master's degree in Boulder, Colorado, called his mother to tell her he was marrying a Jewish woman. Immediately, my sister called me and quietly told me the news. At the time, both of us were extremely conservative Christians, and we were a little taken aback by the news. Neither of us had any qualms about Glen marrying a Jewish woman, but both of us thought immediately of the children. They might never know Jesus, never attend church, my sister and I agonized to each other. We consoled ourselves thinking that God might be bringing Zoe into our lives so we could have an influence on her.

Well, not exactly.

Over the years, Peggy and I have attended seders and Hanukkah parties that Zoe elaborately conducted. We've learned about Judaism through her. Glen and Zoe's son, who was born three years ago, attends Hebrew school, and Peggy and I visit his classroom and watch him as he performs skits and songs with other children at the school.

Before my dad died, he spent hours in his garage handmaking a menorah for Zoe, though he'd lived in a coal-mining town nearly all of his eighty-eight years and had known few, if any, Jews. My brother-in-law, who never dreamed he'd don a yarmulke, often did exactly that, celebrating Jewish holidays and bragging to everyone who crossed his path that his grandson, only three years old, could speak both English and Hebrew (this was, of course, an exaggeration).

Our families became friends, sharing sorrows as well as laughter. At Eliot's bris (the ritual circumcision performed on the tenth day after a boy is born and an occasion that family members and close friends attend), Peggy jokingly whispered to Lloyd, Zoe's dad,

"There has to be something in our religion to get even with you guys for this."

Recently, Peggy and I were talking about how we'd changed over the years. "I guess God put Zoe in our lives to be an influence on *us*," Peggy said. We smiled at our own naivety. Zoe had been the first to introduce us to Judaism, to make us think about other people's spirituality, and to begin to understand that Christians do not have the final say-so on God and on how to know him.

It's something, at least, for Jews to think about.

Times, they are changing. In October 1965, the Second Vatican Council, led by Pope John XIII, issued the historical *Nostra Aetate,* which gave several declarations, including the statements that the "Church rejected any representation of the Jews as repudiated or cursed by God" and that it rejected a theology of an "outdated and superseded Judaism," instead, moving toward a "theology of a living Judaism."

This is an incredible document, undoubtedly reflecting one of the greatest changes in Catholicism toward Judaism ever made. Although Rudy Baum, during the interfaith service, stated that John Paul II has done more than anyone in history to bring about reconciliation, surely John XIII brought in the tide.

Vatican II has been followed by other major shifts in Catholic-Jewish relations. In 1974, Pope Paul VI established the "Pontifical Commission for Religious Relations with the Jews" in order to bring about practical applications of the Vatican's statement nearly ten years earlier. In 1986, Pope John Paul II visited the Great Synagogue in Rome, displaying to the world his acknowledgment of Catholicism's respect for Judaism.

Since then, the Catholic Church has issued statements of apology for their silence during the Holocaust and has made efforts, such as the one I described at the beginning of this chapter, to bring about permanent reminders for the church. Finally, in March 2000, the Pope made a pilgrimage to Israel, where he prayed at the Yad VaShem, Israel's Holocaust memorial. He concluded his visit by placing a prayer at the Western Wall, "begging God's forgiveness for Christian sins against Jews over the centuries."

Because of the hierarchical structure of the Catholic church and its tremendous size, it's difficult for other denominations to make such sweeping statements, but many in the church are moving away from the idea that God has rejected Israel and chosen a new bride, the church.

In *Jews & Christians: A Troubled Family,* Walter Harrelson writes of what describes, for some of us, our past attitude toward Judaism and the church. From earliest times, he writes, Christians have read about the Hebrews' faithlessness. Then they've used this as evidence that God has rejected the Jews and replaced them with a new, faithful people—the Christians!

Harrelson reminds us that Christians who point to the Jews' wavering efforts to serve God overlook an equally important fact: the Jews were among the "most moral and just of ancient peoples," and their history is also one of intense devotion and great fervor in their love for and service to God.[12]

Thankfully, many Christians are reassessing their view of exclusivity and, because of that, Jews are beginning to feel more comfortable around Christians. In the wake of the crisis in the Catholic church, for instance, which surrounded a number of pedophile priests, the Jewish newspaper *Forward* printed an editorial that encouraged Jews to remember their friendship with the Catholic Church. "Catholics . . . have dramatically reconsidered their attitudes toward Jews and Judaism over the last generation, and we can show our appreciation now by showing sympathy for our friends in their pain," the unidentified writer states. "We know what it means to be a faith community on the defensive, to circle the communal wagons around an embattled leadership that's under worldwide assault as it tries to muddle through a crisis it never wished for and can't find its way out of."[13]

Some Jewish groups have struck up a friendship with evangelical church leaders, though others have mixed feelings about the relationship. Conservative Christians, they say, only support Israel because they believe that the return of Jews to Israel will usher in the second coming of Christ.

For certain Jews, though, motives don't matter, as long as Christians aren't proselytizing. It's the support of and love for Israel that matters.

In addition, because many Christians don't hold to a conservative end-times view, their love for Israel stems purely from the fact that we share a testament and a history. As Rabbi Daniel Lapin points out, many Christians love Israel, not because they are obsessed with Armageddon but because they "read the Bible from page one, as we do."[14]

Support of Israel, though, represents only a tiny part of what many Christians and Jews have in common. As I've studied and worshiped with the Jews, for instance, I've noticed that our "law and love" distinctions aren't that distinct at all.

For one thing, the Bible doesn't indicate that love as the center of religion began with Jesus. Rather, it demonstrates that it began with the Jews. The Hebrew scriptures reveal a love story unparalleled in sacred literature, and although Judaism sees ritual as a means to draw closer to God, it also has a deep understanding of love and grace. Indeed, no faith, no religious people, have a more vibrant relationship or a greater intimacy with their God.

On the flip side, I've come to see that Jesus didn't do away with the law. He observed it. He taught it. He sought to get at its heart, arguing in the traditional way of the rabbis and prophets, pounding home the message of social justice and forgiveness and the importance of remembering those who are less fortunate. Jesus, in keeping with the essence of Judaism, sought to establish a godly kingdom on earth.

Although Christianity sees itself as the religion of grace and love, it is, in practice, a religion that understands the importance of ritual and obedience (read "law") in everyday life. The Apostle Paul asked this question: "Do we, then, nullify the law by this faith?" and answers adamantly, "Not at all! Rather, we uphold the law" (Romans 3:31 NIV).

One day, to prepare for an article I was writing, I made a trip to the bookstore to purchase some Christian books on love. Although I scanned the titles of probably two hundred books, I was shocked to find only a few on love and grace. I did, however, find numerous Christian books describing disciplines written to help us develop a deeper and closer walk with God. Christians, both in principle and in practice, revere ritual and law.

As I've become involved with Judaism, I've seen that many of our differences have simply developed apart from the essences of our religions, diverging through time, becoming solidified by popular but misled scholars and religious leaders. Although there are truly differences among our religions, there are also many, many similarities: our belief in a God of love and great passion; our respect for moral law, social justice, and rituals (though they differ) in moving close to God; and our mutual respect of and love for the Hebrew scriptures.

A couple of years ago, NBC's television show *Nightline* ran a story about a Hungarian community, Arad, in which a small, dying Jewish population lived among a larger community of Christians. Mostly, the remaining Jews lived in an "old age home," funded by the American Jewish community, simply because they believed they should be allowed to die in the town they'd always called home.

As Hanukkah drew close, a Christian decided that his Jewish friends deserved to celebrate their holiday in style. He had noticed that the old synagogue sat filthy and unused, so he gathered together a group of townspeople who cleaned and decorated the synagogue. The children at the music school, though none of them were Jewish, trained for many days learning Hebrew songs.

On the day of the holiday, a rabbi drove forty miles to lead the celebration, and a Jewish choir came from a nearby town. However, the synagogue was filled mostly with non-Jews, including the Orthodox bishop, who had come to help the small, remaining Jewish community remember happier times.[15]

When I watched this story, I thought of something I'd read once—that if you truly love Jews, you will help them to become more Jewish. That is exactly what these Romanian Christians did. I also found myself hoping, though, that these Christians had absorbed some of the beauty of Judaism for themselves, that they worshiped God in perhaps a new way, that the Hebrew songs they brought to the synagogue bound them in a closer way to the roots of their own faith.

During the festival of Sukkot, it's traditional to ritually wave with the right hand what's known as a *lulav,* or palm branch, along with the *hadassim,* or myrtle-branch and the *aravot,* or willow-branch. In the left hand is held a lemonlike fruit called the *etrog.*

151

Each of the branches might be seen as a representation of unity. The leaves of the *lulav* must be unopened and bound together. The three leaves of the *hadassim* must grow out of one stem. And the willow-branch, which is also called *achvana,* represents brotherly love. Though each of these resonates with an image of unity in and of itself, the portrait that emerges when they're bound together is even more powerful. That evening, I couldn't help but hope that the three branches—the *lulav,* the *hadassim,* and the *achvana*—bound together might one day reflect the three branches of faith that have emerged from Abraham.

The evening I attended Sukkot at Hesha's, each of us stood with the *lulav* as Joseph, the *gabbai* of the congregation, showed us how to wave it. Traditionally, the *lulav* is waved in six directions, first toward the east, then south, west, north, above, and, finally, below. Joseph, however, had us wave it in one last direction, where it rested—upon the heart. This, I have come to realize, is indeed where unity must begin.

CHAPTER EIGHT

A Spiritual Journey

There's a traditional Jewish tale about an old Hasidic rabbi who crossed the village square every morning on his way to the temple to pray. One morning, a Cossack soldier who was feeling particularly cranky approached the rabbi and asked him where he was going.

"I don't know," replied the rabbi.

"What do you mean you don't know?" said the soldier, furiously. "You've crossed the town square every morning for twenty-five years! How dare you toy with me? Now tell me where you're going!"

The rabbi insisted he didn't know.

The soldier, feeling slighted and ridiculed, grabbed the rabbi by his coat and dragged him off to jail.

"See?" the rabbi said as the soldier opened the cell doors and gave him a shove. "I told you I didn't know where I was going."[1]

When I first read this story, I thought to myself how indicative this is of a spiritual journey. Unless we've closed our minds to all questions and to lessons from other faiths, we really don't know with any degree of certainty where we're going. Ten years ago, I had no idea that I'd become so captivated by Judaism and so in love with its rituals, its teachings, its mysticism—and its people.

Most of my friends and family noticed my love. "Happy Hanukkah," my nephew e-mailed me a couple of years ago. "Have you checked your genealogy?" a friend in my Sunday school class asked me. One evening, when I missed my weekly study with Rabbi G. and showed up at home early, my husband asked me if I had decided to convert to Christianity.

When I first began this book, I wasn't certain how I was going to approach the concluding chapter. But when I mentioned it to my friends, both Jewish and Christian, almost all expressed a desire to know where I was, at the present time, in my spiritual journey regarding Judaism and Christianity. Was I considering converting to Judaism? Had I decided to remain in the church? Or was I vacillating?

Over the years, I've thought frequently of converting. Judaism fulfills so many needs in me and so utterly fascinates me that it's often agonizing to me to love it so much without being a complete part of it. Not long ago, as the Jewish High Holy Days approached, I was at a gathering of women celebrating Rosh Chodesh when a woman who had recently converted told the group that this would be her first High Holiday as a Jew. Her face glowed as another woman present reminisced with her about her recent conversion. "I'll never forget when you were about to be immersed into the *mikvah* [a cleansing ritual] and you suddenly turned around and shouted, 'I'm a Jew!'"

When I heard this, I felt envious.

However, in my vacillating, I've continued to find much that I still love about Christianity and about Jesus. I attend a fabulous church, feel a great deal of closeness with my Sunday school class, and have an outstanding pastor who continues to expand my ideas of God and spirituality in unique ways. Because I've attended church since I was two weeks old, the church feels like home.

I also have a great deal of spiritual freedom where I am. Were I to become a Jew, I feel I'd have to throw myself heart and soul into that faith tradition, when what I want in my life right now is to throw myself heart and soul into experiencing God in as many ways as I can. It's only been in the past several years that I've even felt this freedom.

In each journey in life, you must be where you are, advises Tzvi Freeman. You may only be passing through on your way to somewhere else seemingly more important; nevertheless, there is purpose in where you are right now.[2] I do indeed feel that sense of purpose where I am.

I have other reservations. I can't imagine myself as a Jew freely loving Christianity, though as a Christian I can love Judaism as deeply and passionately as I want. I don't know if this is true or not, but it's the way I feel.

As I've struggled, both my Jewish and Christian friends have been there for me. People neither judge nor pull me. Many of my Jewish friends are simply grateful for the path I'm on and that I've felt the need to tell about it.

Not long ago, Hesha invited me to her home, along with a small group of other men and women, because she was hosting a Hasidic rabbi from Israel. The rabbi was traveling through the United States in order to raise money to aid the poor in the Ashdod area of Israel. Hesha's teenage daughter Danielle stood at the front door as we entered, reminding us, in whispers, that the rabbi was Orthodox and that we shouldn't try to shake his hand.

Before the others arrived, four of us sat at the kitchen table while the rabbi finished a meal that Hesha had prepared for him. One of Danielle's friends, a Christian teenager, asked Hesha if she could come into the kitchen for a moment so she could see the "holy man from Israel." How fascinated we Christians are, I thought. The rabbi, however, was confused by her interest. "Does she have a Jewish parent?" he asked Hesha. Hesha told him she didn't. Danielle's friend waved shyly and scampered from the room.

Right off the bat, the rabbi wanted to know if I was Jewish and why, since I obviously loved Judaism, I didn't convert. Was it fear, he wondered?

Soon he and Hesha lapsed into conversations in Hebrew (he spoke only faltering, broken English), and after a while both agreed that I was a "messenger."

"That's why I've never pushed you to convert," Hesha said. "I always knew that you had a message for the Christian world."

Only one person, whom I don't know well, expressed reservations about a Christian writing a book on Judaism. "If you're going to represent the Jewish people," she told me, "then you need to join us and represent us as a Jew." I understood her concern, but my experience with Judaism has been one I've had as a Christian, and I can only tell about it through those eyes.

How unprepared I was for this passionate love affair with a faith that six or seven years ago I knew virtually nothing about. No one who knows me doubts the depth of my love for Judaism.

Recently, I attended a Tisha b'Av service with my friend Karen at a Conservative synagogue, Congregation Beth Torah. Tisha b'Av commemorates the day that the second Temple was destroyed and, traditionally, the day the first Temple was destroyed also.

After a brief service, the lights were extinguished, and our small group of about a dozen sat on the floor, each of us holding a candle. One of Karen's friends, Eleanor Eidels, chanted the first few lines of the book of Lamentations in a beautiful soprano voice, then we went around the room, each of us reading several verses of the first chapter until we'd reached its end. As we moved to the second chapter, Eleanor again chanted the first few verses, then we read chapter two, and so on until we'd read the entire book.

I had read through the book of Lamentations several times and knew its history, but it's difficult to explain what happened to me that evening. For the first time in all the times I'd read Lamentations, I felt the pain of the Jews over the loss of their Temple. In spirit, I mourned with those who stood daily at the Western Wall. As we read the book of Lamentations that night, I did so not with a mere knowledge of Jewish history but with the heart of a Jew.

The Old Testament has become, for me, the Testament of the Hebrews, and this is vastly more than a simple name change. Rather, it's a newly found respect for Jewish ritual and law and a broader understanding of its beauty and significance. Realizing that the Hebrew scriptures are about the Hebrews (again, how embarrassing that I ever thought otherwise) gives me a feeling of awe at being in the presence of the Jews. What a tremendous gift they have given the world in the pages of scripture and what a glorious God they have revealed.

In his lovely book *The Gifts of the Jews,* Thomas Cahill points out that the Jews have influenced Western society in every conceivable way. "Without the Jews," he writes, "we would see the world through different eyes, hear with different ears, even feel with different feelings. . . . we would think with a different mind, interpret all our experience differently, draw different conclusions from the things that befall us. And we would set a different course for our lives."[3]

Although Jewish thought has permeated Western society, the church has a long way to go in embracing this spiritually. How unfortunate for us that the earliest "New Testament" manuscripts have only been preserved in Greek rather than in the Aramaic language that Jesus and his disciples spoke—a language that uses the Hebrew alphabet and is interpreted in much the same manner. Greek isn't merely a language barrier; it's an obstacle to an accurate understanding of the Semitic nature of the New Testament.

In *Hebrew Thought Compared with Greek,* scholar and writer Thorleif Boman writes that these two languages are in their very essence different. The images and thinking associated with each result in distinctive conclusions and interpretations. Hebrew thinking is dynamic, he writes, while Greek is static. The Semites were "dynamic, vigorous, passionate and sometimes quite explosive" while the Greeks were "peaceful, moderate, and harmonious." And the idiosyncrasies of each show up in their language.[4]

When I first began to grasp the significance of these differences, I began fanatically doing word studies, comparing and contrasting the two languages, trying to get a better feel of Semitic thought by trying to figure out what specific words Jesus might have been using and what they would have meant to his listeners. I bought a Pashita Bible (a translation from ancient Aramaic texts), still used by Christians in the East who think more mystically than do Christians of the West.

Finally, though, I realized that this was basically futile. A Jewish friend explained that as I better understood Judaism and Semitic thought in general, I would better understand the message of the Christian Bible in its entirety without having to struggle with what specific words might have been used. Grasping the context and Semitic thought and traditions that lay *behind* the words would be more helpful, he said, in altering my interpretations of the Westernized and Greek-influenced Christian Testament.

This has proved to be true and helpful.

In addition to profoundly affecting the way I read scripture, though, the Jews have made me a more deeply spiritual person. This year, during the Jewish High Holidays, I have a *chevruta,* a study partner—my friend Karen. We're meditating privately using a devotional book that Roz Katz and other Rosh Chodesh members put together, and then we meet and talk about our lives, the changes we want to make, and the ways that God is moving and transforming us. The month of *Elul,* which precedes the High Holidays, is the time for self-reflection, for repentance, for forgiving others, and asking forgiveness of any you've wronged.

As I've worked through the meditations and prayed for guidance in this realm, expecting to dredge up the same old people with whom I continually have personality conflicts, I was surprised to find that there were others whom I needed to forgive. After one meditation, I worked through a problem with someone I'd been avoiding because of the pain she'd unknowingly caused me.

A few weeks ago, during our first meeting, another friend, Nancy Jellinek, joined us for lunch, and the three of us lost track of time as we shared our private struggles and encouraged one another in our efforts to work through them. Afterward we stood in the parking lot of the restaurant, and Nancy and Karen sang a blessing for me in Hebrew—the blessing that accompanies completing a project because I'd just finished my first draft of this book.

The spirituality of my Jewish friends has deeply touched my life and moved me to want to incorporate many aspects of their faith into my own spiritual life. Hesha, for instance, is in a year-long sabbatical from teaching in order to work through issues in her life that she feels need to be taken care of before she can be a fully effective spiritual leader. Although I've tried repeatedly to make her feel guilty for withholding her incredible gifts from the world (I miss her terribly), I also know that when she returns to leadership, it will be with a new depth.

I've absorbed other spiritual lessons from the Jews. I remember a story that Rabbi G. told one evening about a Hasid who, every Sabbath, would lie on his back in the doorway of the synagogue. People would step over him and come inside to pray, and he would continue to lie there. It was a symbol of humility, the Hasid said, a reminder that he was no better than a doormat.

Week after week he did this, Rabbi G. said, and finally, one day, another Hasid came in and stepped on him, wiping his feet on the man's back. Immediately, the Hasid jumped up and shouted at him, "Hey! What are you doing? Can't you see I'm lying here?"

"Well," the other Hasid said, "I thought you were a doormat. If you're a doormat, I'm supposed to wipe my feet on you."

This story, said Rabbi G., tells us that if you're trying to show off your humility, then it's not true humility at all.

Rabbi G. has, for me, been a lovely example of true humility. One night, as Sasha was telling Rabbi G. how he had changed his life, the rabbi interrupted him. "No," he said, "you have changed your life. Give yourself credit. Only honor me by coming to my funeral. But just cry a little. Not much."

My friend Kati Pressman, who opened her home to me during the Torah retreat in Colorado, wrote two lovely books in which she poetically describes this imperfect struggle for humility:

Reaching for our divinity
praying for humility—
Our "huminity"
keeps us in balance.[5]

How deeply the Jews have affected my life. My God is more magnificent, my spirituality deeper, my prayer life richer. I have become so intertwined with Judaism that in church I often open my Christian Bible backwards, expecting to find the book of Genesis, and being startled by the sight of the book of Revelation. (Hebrew is read from left to right, and Hebrew texts open from what is, to us, the back of the book.)

Now I take my Tanakh to church, so I can read along in the Hebrew scriptures when the Old Testament is read aloud, noting the differences and similarities, absorbing the Hebrew atmosphere of the Bible, even in church.

People often express amazement at my complete comfort at Jewish gatherings, even Orthodox and Hasidic ones, when I'm almost always the only non-Jew present. Once, a reporter was doing a story for a local tabloid, the *Dallas Observer,* and spent a couple of evenings with us at Ruach Torah. When she realized that I wasn't Jewish, she called to interview me.

At one point during the service that the reporter had attended, Hesha had asked us to look deeply into the eyes of the person sitting next to us and to imagine that we had been together, in spirit, at Mount Sinai, standing before Moses as he received and passed on the commandments that would bind the Jewish people and influence the entire world.

"Didn't you feel odd and left out, being non-Jewish?" asked the reporter.

I told her I didn't, that I felt a communion with the Jewish people that was very mystical in its nature.

"So don't you get in arguments about Jesus?" she pressed me.

"Never," I said. "That's not what I'm there for. I'm there to learn from *them* and to broaden my own understanding of God and faith."

"I just can't believe that," the reporter said.

"It's true," I told her.

Recently, I was walking through my neighborhood when I noticed three children sitting in a car in a driveway, apparently waiting for one of their parents to drive them somewhere. As I passed by, a little boy called out at the top of his voice, "Hiiiiii!"

"Hiiiii!" I called back.

"Who that?" one of the other children sitting in the car asked him.

"She my friend," he told her, then turning to me, he called out loudly, "You my friend?"

"I'm your friend!" I called back.

"See," he said, turning back to the little girl, "Told you."

Although he was black, young, and male, and I am white, older, and female, we became, abruptly, mystically, spontaneously, friends.

And this was what I wanted the reporter to understand. They're Jews; I'm gentile. But abruptly, mystically, spontaneously, we've become friends. Were she to spend several weeks with us, she'd understand. "See?" I'd say to her. "Told you."

For the first couple of years after I began studying and worshiping with the Jews, I tried to hide the fact that I was a Christian. For the most part, I simply didn't want people treating me differently, changing the way they conversed and interacted with one another.

I was thrilled, for instance, when a man handed me a tract on what to do if I were approached by a Christian missionary. I thought this was really insider information. Had they known I was a Christian, they would never have believed my intentions were sincere, I thought, and they would have waited until I had left before they handed such contraband literature out.

My intentions, of course, *were* sincere. I had been sheltered within a conservative Christian environment for so many years that I had no idea—and had never before cared—how people of other religions felt. Now I cared very much.

Yet how humorous my secretiveness seems to me now. My Jewish friends have never hidden the way they feel about being targeted for evangelism and, from time to time, I've received material through the mail, announcing seminars and conferences designed to teach Jews how to respond to Christian missionaries. The best-known speaker on this subject is Rabbi Tovia Singer, who directs *Outreach Judaism* and travels extensively, appearing regularly on television and radio shows, in his efforts to help young Jews answer Christian missionaries and find a more solid backing for their own faith.

Had I wanted to know how Jews feel about this subject, I could have simply asked any one of them and they would have been happy to tell me. I didn't have to try and hide my Christian identity to find out.

Indeed, when I began to feel comfortable *not* trying to hide who I was, I didn't feel out of place at all. In fact, I felt *more* accepted, perhaps because I was being open and honest, and people began to sense my sincerity rather than feel I was trying to hide something from them. The rejection I feared almost never came.

Occasionally, the revelations were humorous. During my early months of study with the Jews, I was, one evening, sitting with an older woman in the lobby of the Jewish Community Center waiting for Reid to unlock the library door and to begin our study, when she suddenly asked me where I went to *shul* (synagogue). At the time, I had no idea what a *shul* was and had to confess to her that I wasn't Jewish.

"I knoooowwwww," she said, looking at me like one of those psychic personalities on TV. "I knooooow."

"How do you know?" I asked.

"You don't have that looook."

On rare occasions, I did wish that I could've better hidden my Christianity. Once, before the study began, a couple of people were discussing how Christianity in general interprets some of the Hebrew prophets, believing that many of their words point to Jesus. As they talked about it, they became more and more heated and angry. Suddenly, one of them turned toward me and nearly shouted, "You people have got it wrong!"

I was stunned and embarrassed. I had only been coming to the study for a couple of months and had already become utterly infatuated with Judaism. I wanted to learn from the Jews, to reassess what I'd been taught; I certainly didn't want to debate. "Stop accusing her as if she's done anything," an elderly man wearing a *kippah* said to the angry woman.

I thought I was going to cry, which embarrassed me all the more. I finally excused myself and went to the restroom to get a grip. When I returned, the study had begun and, after it was over, the angry woman came up to me. "I'm so sorry if I embarrassed you," she said. "I didn't mean to." An elderly man approached me and asked me if he had interrupted me at some point during the study and, if so, he was very sorry.

Later, I would understand this woman's anger, feeling with her—and all the Jews—the unsavory history of Christian attitudes and persecutions and forced conversions and prejudice and fervent evangelism. And she would come to understand why I was there and that my intentions were pure. During the two years I regularly studied with the group, there were no more incidents like this one.

As I became more involved in Judaism, however, I still sometimes hid my faith because I wanted to fit in. Judaism was permeating who I was, changing my faith and my concept of God; I wanted to be part of them.

Again, I came to realize that it wasn't necessary for me to play games in order to do this. Everywhere I've worshiped, the Jews have welcomed me and made me feel a part, knowing that I wasn't.

At Ruach Torah, Hesha considered Mike and me part of an inner circle, confiding what she believed to be mysteries of the faith and drawing us fully into everything she did. She assured us that she loved and accepted us whether we remained Christians or converted to Judaism.

That I felt part of more ideologically liberal groups, though, isn't as astounding as the fact that I've also felt part of the Orthodox, particularly the Hasidim. Always, the little group I studied with for so many years embraced me, expressing an interest in my life, my struggles, and my thoughts about God.

Rabbi G. used language that always made me feel included. "The rabbis and *other ministers*," he'd say, or "Jews and *other godly people*," "synagogues and *other houses of worship*." If I arrived early and he had finished his prayers, he'd sit and talk to me, sometimes asking questions about my life. One night, when I was leaving, I spontaneously turned and told the group I loved them. "We love you, too!" Sasha said without hesitation.

When I found out my dad had terminal cancer, I received a note from Rabbi G., which I still have. "Hi Merry," it read [I loved the accidental play on my name], "I am very sorry to hear that your father is so ill. I just want to give you my blessings for his speedy recovery and we should hear only good news, and you should have the strength to deal with all this."

When my dad passed away, Hesha had a tree planted in Israel in his memory, and another friend gave me his prayer book and showed me how to recite *Kaddish*—the Jewish prayer said in synagogue each day for a year, then each year on the person's *yahrzeit,* or day of passing, after a close family member's death. Mystically, this prayer is supposed to elevate the soul of the loved one, bringing him or her into a closer, more ecstatic union with God. I set up a small altar in my office, bought a candle and, on special days connected in some way with my dad, I light the candle and recite the prayer, first in English, then in Hebrew.

All of these friends have become so precious to me, and I'm grateful that they've come to love me, also. Although I'm still a Christian, I've fallen deeply in love with Judaism, often feeling, as the song goes, torn between two lovers. Secretly, I hope that Hesha and Marc and other friends are right—that I really do have a Jewish *neshama,* a Jewish soul. For I want, in the deepest part of my being, to be a genuine part.

One very late evening at Ruach Torah, after a long and extraordinary prayer service in which the dirty dishes from our potluck still sat on the table, Hesha asked us to quietly clear the table and, as we felt moved, to bless at least three people. The room was charged with spiritual energy, as it always was, and Hesha was encouraging us not to destroy it with superficial chatter but to cap the atmosphere with additional acts of holiness and worship.

"Look deeply into the eyes of the person you're blessing," said Hesha. "If you're uncomfortable," she added with a shrug of her shoulders and a lift of her hands, "that's OK! Be uncomfortable! Do it anyway!"

As one of my friends approached me, he gripped my shoulders, explaining that this was the way the ancient rabbis were said to bless another. The blessing was lengthy and profound, and I felt my eyes tearing. For most of us who had spent a lot of intimate time together, the blessings were affirmations of caring and love, and the connection, as we stood facing one another, was deep and intense.

"A blessing," writes Rachel Naomi Remen, "is not something that one person gives another. A blessing is a moment of meeting, a certain kind of relationship in which both people involved remember and acknowledge their true nature and worth, and strengthen what is whole in one another."[6] It was clear that we all instinctively knew this as we embraced and affirmed—blessed—each person we passed, each one whom we'd come to know and love.

That was, however, one of our rare quiet nights at Ruach Torah. Most nights were filled with such an exuberance and wild joy that I often suspected that the very walls pulsated with spiritual energy.

Two of the songs we used to sing seemed to be everyone's favorites. One of them had several verses that we'd sing enthusiastically. Then, as the chorus approached, Hesha would raise her hands high in the air and bring them down on the table with a resounding bang. *"Dai dai dai dai dai,"* we'd sing, all of us pounding the table in unison, irresistibly catching Hesha's lovely and vibrant spirit.

In the other song, Hesha had the men stand together, linking arms in sideways embraces and joyfully and exuberantly, often at the top of their voices, chanting a series of blessings; the women, with equal enthusiasm, sang a repetitive chorus.

"Bless this place, and all who have shared our meal," the men would chant. "May the food we eat, strengthen the love we feel." And the women would, during the chant, sing simultaneously, in loud and joyful praise, *"Ha-Rachaman, Ha-Rachaman"* (O Holy One of Compassion).

Bless the One, who blesses us with peace,
May our will to do your work increase.
Bless the child, who searches for you in vain,
May the suffering ones find respite from their pain.
Bless our friends, who have so much to bear,
May the homeless folk find shelter in your care.[7]

My husband, who had, in the beginning, been so shy about being around these enthusiastic Jews, now stood linked with them, swaying as they did, a *kippah* perched atop his head, in complete comfort.

"Sing loudly enough that the neighbors will hear!" Hesha said, slapping the table. "Sing loudly enough that they'll hear and catch our spiritual joy and energy!"

Personally, I didn't see how anyone could miss it.

AFTERWORD

The great Jewish theologian, Martin Buber once wisely observed that religions are like houses of worship and that you can only look through the windows *from the outside* of those other than your own. Mary Blye Howe comes disturbingly close to proving him wrong. She is clearly a Baptist but she has peered through the windows of so many different Jewish prayer halls that she has acquired a remarkably clear vision of American Judaism. Or, to put it another way, Ms. Howe seems simply to have done it all and got it right.

She has hung around enough of the right Jews, asked enough of the right questions, brought with her enough of her own native spiritual sophistication and been blessed with a facility for religious language to provide us with an insightful, refreshing, and important window into the spiritual vitality of American Judaism—and as she illustrates, spiritual vitality can transcend denominational and even faith traditions.

I must confess, I initially opened the manuscript of *A Baptist Among the Jews* with some trepidation, fearing that it would be uninformed or, worse, false advertising. This reader is relieved to report, however, that Ms. Howe's book is both accurate and neutral. It does not shrink from either identifying Judaism's foibles or exulting its beauties. The book is, in other words, *kosher*—religiously fit, acceptable, proper, correct. For Christians it is a kind of Lewis and Clark report of a mission of exploration. For Jews, it is a book about how we look from the outside. Indeed, I only hope it will receive the kind of attention in the Jewish community it also deserves and that more Christians (and a few Jews too!) could have courage and good fortune to have experiences similar to Howe's at their local synagogue.

Mary Blye Howe reminds us that Judaism is not so much a faith as it is a people, and a people with a diverse, rich, and frequently cacophonous collection of spiritual practices and traditions. Obviously, Jews do believe things—everybody does. But in Judaism, beliefs do not get organized, rehearsed, or (probably because they are so mercurial in the first place) become very important to Jewish religiosity. Moses Maimonides, arguably one of the wisest Jews who ever lived, tried to come up with a list of what Jews should believe. He identified thirteen "articles of faith." Alas, he couldn't find more than a half dozen Jews who agreed with more than seven of them. So, they made it into a song called, *"Yigdal"* and put it into the prayer book.

I once had a professor in rabbinic school, Dr. Samuel Sandmel, who used to caution us: "Gentlemen (in those days it was only men), if you don't seriously doubt the existence of God every few weeks, you are theologically comatose!" For us Jews, beliefs come and go and the holiest (and hardest) thing you can do is simply to tell yourself the truth. When, as a congregational rabbi, I used to work with students toward conversion to Judaism who had come from a Christian tradition, I would have to remind them that they were not doing a re-tread on their souls, or even changing religions. They were becoming members of a people. Their conversion meant that they would be stuck with the Jewish people and the Jewish people would be stuck with them. What they believed (short of, Jesus being their personal savior) was simply not all that important.

Ms. Howe also lays to rest what is perhaps one of the strangest stereotypes in the strange (and often too intimate) history of Jewish-Christian relations. Apparently by mutual consent, Christianity defined itself as a religion of love and Judaism defined itself as a religion of law. (Christians: "You can have the law, well we take love!" or, Jews: "You claim God is too demanding because you don't have enough conviction to live by what God wants!") So, Jesus, it was agreed, preached love while the Jews upheld the law. But, of course, it was not only silly, it was inaccurate. Jesus followed and taught the Law of Moses and the Jews understand that love is always the goal, even though it probably cannot be legislated in an unredeemed world. The word *Torah* itself (which is Hebrew for *the Five Books of Moses*) was claimed to mean "law." This meant, supposedly, that Jews were faithful to the Mosaic Law which Christians, for their part, became convinced was superceded by Christian love. In its most extreme forms (depending, of course, on your side of the debate), the law-love controversy portrayed Christians as antinomian anarchists or Jews as slaving, unfeeling legalists incapable of affection. Some people, inclined to fiercer formulations, became convinced that the God of the Hebrew Bible was vengeful and legalistic or that the God of the New Testament was unaware of humanity's this-worldly need for structure or even justice. Of course it's all nonsense and properly belongs in the theological trash bin of foolish ideas. Jews (what a surprise!) are fully capable of love, giving and receiving it many times a day and

Christians (astonishing!) lead lives of legal precision and devotion to religious structure.

While, as a rabbi, I am sorry Judaism has "lost" a soul with as much obvious spiritual depth as Ms. Howe's, I am comforted that she will be able to continue her search and teaching among the people of her birth. Reminding people—Christian, Moslem, or Jew—that they do not enjoy a monopoly on holiness or "the way to Heaven" is usually a thankless project but it is vital and holy nonetheless. And many of us now have the increasingly focused sense that, in the coming century, it may actually become an act of politics as much as religion.

Rabbi Lawrence Kushner

JUDAISM 101

O f the seven types of synagogues, I've been privileged to study
or worship at all but one (Reconstructionist). I've entered
the women's door and sat in exclusion in order to worship with the
Orthodox, banged tables and sung with the Jews of Jewish
Renewal, studied and worshiped with the Hasidim, and lost myself
in worship at Reform and Traditional synagogues.

My goal in writing this book was to share my experiences—
to give you the privilege of eavesdropping on the Jews' exuberant arguments with God, absorbing some of their comfort with
mystery, becoming engaged in their endless fascination with spiritual study, participating in their limitless exploration of the
nature of God, and becoming drawn in by the rich symbolism of
their prayer and ritual. I have wanted you to come to know the
Jews.

This section, however, will allow you to understand a bit more
about the different types of synagogues (or different movements)
within Judaism.[1] Basically, there are seven: the most liberal ideologically are Jewish Renewal, Reform, and Reconstructionist;
Conservative hovers somewhat in the middle; Traditional,

Orthodox, and the Hasidim are strict in both their ritual observance and their ideology.

Here is what you might encounter when attending any one of these services and what you should know about their beliefs and practices.

Jewish Renewal

The newest movement in Judaism is Jewish Renewal. Jewish Renewal groups are formed as *havurahs*—small groups that meet in a rented room at a synagogue affiliated with another branch of Judaism or in a home. Often, those involved in Jewish Renewal are also active members of a synagogue. Ruach Torah—the group I worshiped and studied with for several years and led by Hesha Abrams—was a Jewish Renewal *havurah*.

Jewish Renewal was begun by Rabbi Zalman Schachter-Shalomi and Rabbi Shlomo Carlebach. Both trained as Lubavitchers but left Hasidism in order to found a movement meant to infuse Judaism with a deeper spirituality. Its emphasis, according to ALEPH, the Alliance for Jewish Renewal, is on "direct spiritual experience and mystical or Kabbalistic teachings."[2]

Services are usually charismatic and exuberant, though this depends on the personality of the leadership. The havurah I regularly attended was extremely vibrant. One of my Jewish friends teased Hesha about being a reincarnated Church of God minister, but there's really no resemblance. Jewishness permeates these havurahs in observance, tradition, festivals, study, and ideology.

Unlike a synagogue, which closely follows one of many Jewish prayer books, there's no hard-and-fast order to most Jewish Renewal services. Ruach Torah compiled their own songs and prayers and used them randomly, as the "spirit" led. Indeed, another facet of Jewish Renewal is the effort to bring "joy and creativity" to spiritual practice.

Membership at Ruach Torah varied to an extreme. One couple attended a Traditional synagogue, whose ideology closely resembles Orthodox, whereas others didn't attend synagogue at all. One member was drawn to the mystical elements in Jewish Renewal; another loved the deep spirituality the movement often exudes.

Hesha herself observed the laws and rituals of Judaism rather carefully, as did Joseph, the *gabbai* (rabbinical assistant). Potluck meals were vegetarian, and no non-kosher food was allowed inside the homes in which we met. Although the leadership wasn't overly cautious about some of the more strict laws of Judaism, they did observe as closely as they could.

Currently, there are about fifty known Jewish Renewal havurahs around the United States, as well as several others in countries such as Brazil, Canada, Israel, and Switzerland.

The length of services varies widely. Ruach Torah's often lasted from 6 P.M. until midnight, and I was never ready to go home.

Reform

Of the sects of Judaism with full denominational status, Reform is the largest. The Reform denomination began in Germany in 1809, but by the 1840s, under the leadership of Rabbi I. M. Wise, it began to spread in the United States, eventually becoming the largest Jewish movement in North America. Today, there are more than nine hundred temples in the United States and Canada.

In the beginning, Reformers abandoned many traditional practices, such as wearing the tallit (prayer shawl), keeping kosher, and conducting prayer services in Hebrew. As late as 1955, Reform congregations were still forbidding the use of the tallit in their synagogues.

Early Reform services also included a German sermon, along with choral singing accompanied by an organ—characteristics of the church rather than of Judaism. Talmud, the books that outlined Jewish law, was outdated and had lost its relevance, according to Reform Jews.

The three national conventions that have been held since 1937, however, have seen a steady return to Jewish tradition and ritual. Talmud study has received more attention, and you won't find organs in very many modern Reform synagogues.

Although the denomination itself subscribes to the autonomy of the individual and doesn't require a strict level of ritual observance, there's a fairly strong movement among some Reform Jews to become more observant. They long for more traditional practices and more Hebrew incorporated into their services.

Temple Emanu-El, the largest Reform temple in Dallas, has a small Saturday morning service in their chapel in which more traditional elements are infused into the prayer service. This satisfies many, while others who want the freedom Reform ideology offers along with traditional services sometimes alternate synagogue attendance with Traditional or Orthodox.

I worship at Temple Emanu-El from time to time and always find it intensely spiritual, captivatingly Jewish, and comfortable. The rabbis act as if they have Christians visiting every week, though they certainly don't. They're simply comfortable with Christians. They're the local leaders in interfaith services. Their senior rabbi, David Stern, along with my pastor, hosts public discussions—not debates—and their friendship is warm and real. They care about everyone, not just Jews, and their charity extends in every direction throughout the city.

The Reform movement is unapologetically liberal in its ideology. The level of ritual observance is up to the individual. Participation of women in leadership roles is high, with women serving in all roles, including that of rabbi. In addition, gays and lesbians enjoy full acceptance, at least officially.

In short, although some liberal Jews long for a closer walk with their ancient traditions, very few want the restrictions that accompany a return to Orthodoxy. Thus, as "wandering" Jews continue to return to their own religion, the Reform temples are likely to grow stronger and more prolific in number.

Services at Reform temples are in English and Hebrew, and when Hebrew is used, it's almost always accompanied by a translation. Services follow a prayer book, though their contents vary from denomination to denomination.

On Saturday morning, the Torah scroll is carried down the aisles. People move to the end of the aisle; most touch Torah with their prayer books, then raise the books to their lips to kiss. Prayer shawls are primarily worn by the rabbis, though some Jewish congregants wear them as well. It's okay for a non-Jew to touch Torah, but it isn't okay to wear a prayer shawl.

Services last about an hour, though there is usually Torah study, similar to Christian Sunday school, before Saturday morning services. The Jewish Sabbath begins at sundown Friday night and ends at sundown Saturday night; virtually all synagogues have both Friday night and Saturday morning services.

After prayer service, *Kiddush* (the blessing over wine) is recited outside the sanctuary, in the foyer. *"Le chaim,"* everyone says after the rabbi recites the blessing. "To life!" After this, the rabbi gives a second blessing and everyone eats a piece of challah—a delicious bread favored by Jews because it's mentioned in the Torah. *"Le chaim!"* everyone shouts, then "Good Shabbos!" and people disburse, getting in their cars and driving home or to restaurants.

Reconstructionist

Reconstructionist Judaism is a third liberal branch of Judaism. Like Reform, they believe that Judaism evolves and changes over the years and that Jews must adapt their ideology accordingly. Also like Reform, they're assimilated Jews, accepting of and interested in building relationships with those of other religions while maintaining intense efforts to nurture and build their own. Although Reform is generally regarded as more liberal than Reconstructionist, the practical aspects of their ideology are closely united.

Although Reconstructionism has had a strong influence on American Judaism, it has remained small. There are no synagogues in the Dallas–Fort Worth Metroplex where I live nor in the states surrounding Texas. Were there any services I could catch along a drive to southern Illinois, I asked the Philadelphia Rabbinical Association? Nope. Nor are there any in the states *surrounding* southern Illinois, except for St. Louis, Missouri, and it's a havurah that often has to bring in rabbis outside their own denomination to hold services. Thus, my own experience with Reconstructionist congregations has been nil.

Reconstructionism began in America in the 1920s, led by Rabbi Mordecai M. Kaplan. Kaplan, a rabbi in the Conservative sect of Judaism, professor of homiletics, and principal of the Teachers' Institute of the Jewish Theological Seminary, longed for liberal reform in the more Orthodox branches of Judaism, although his intention, at least initially, wasn't to create a new denomination.

Eventually though, as the tension between his own burgeoning movement and Conservatism grew, Kaplan felt compelled to resign his post as rabbi of the prestigious Jewish Center on Manhattan's upscale West Side, and he, along with thirty-five families, mostly financially successful businessmen and their families, established a new synagogue. Proud to have such an honorable man as their rabbi, the entire congregation would rise when he walked down the aisle on *Shabbat* (Sabbath) morning.

One of the core tenets of Reconstructionism is that Judaism is a "civilization." Judaism is more than a religion or synagogue, believed Kaplan, and "Jewishness" should be infused into all parts of a Jew's life, including art, theater, education, and science. The idea was to give the Jews a strong sense of identity that took them beyond Sabbath worship.

Unlike Reform, Reconstructionism began with a strong sense of Zionism, which advocates the ultimate return of the Jewish people to Eretz Israel, the land of Israel. (Reform is now Zionist, but it didn't begin that way.) Because the first Reconstructionist synagogue still belonged to the Conservative denomination, they were also ritually observant in their services.

Although Rabbi Kaplan believed in and advocated the full participation of women in synagogue life (the first bat mitzvah was introduced at the Society for the Advancement of Judaism for his daughter), women were in reality marginalized. It would be nearly thirty years before Reconstructionist synagogues began counting women in *minyan* (a quorum of ten, which is required to hold a service) and began to be "called to Torah," that is, to read the portion of the week from the Hebrew Torah scroll during worship service.

Reconstructionism also, in its beginning, focused more on the Jewish people than it did on God. Rituals and prayer services were seen more as " 'folkways' which preserved group memories and transmitted fundamental group values," more than they were as a means of connection with God.[3] This changed, however, under the leadership of Arthur Green, who successfully advocated bringing the idea of a personal God back into the movement. Today, Reconstructionism generally has a more "vertical" focus and more emphasis on divine relationship.

Many congregations, because of their small size, meet in homes. Indeed, the idea of the havurah was born in this movement.

Services are often lively and untraditional and, for the most part, are in English or a translation is provided.

Like its liberal counterpart Reform, Reconstructionism appeals to Jews who, by and large, want to keep what they feel is the essence of Judaism without feeling an obligation to practice all of the rituals that the Orthodox observe daily. They believe Judaism has always changed with time and, indeed, if this ancient and holy faith is to survive, they say, it must continue to do so.

Conservative

Not long ago, I attended Shacharit (the morning service) at a Conservative synagogue. Several of us gathered outside, waiting for daylight, so the service could begin. "I think I see a ray of light!" said someone, "unless it's the parking lot of Temple Emanu-El."

It's a typical Conservative joke. The Conservative movement took shape in reaction to the Reform movement, which, in 1885, adopted a platform that regarded Jewish ritual as "relative and dispensable." And although the Reform movement has enjoyed an increasing return to ritual observance, many outside the movement still regard Reform as Judaism-light—a joke that Reform Jews try to take "lightly."

The Conservative movement originated simultaneously in Europe and America in the middle of the nineteenth century and sought to acknowledge and honor certain modern changes in Judaism while retaining traditional rituals and observances.

Although Conservatism made a valiant effort to retain ties with Orthodoxy, the break came when an association of Orthodox synagogues, at its third convention, refused to acknowledge the graduates of the new Jewish Theological Seminary as rabbis. The Conservative movement was forced at that point to define itself in a new way.

At first, Solomon Schechter, a name familiar to most Jews in the Conservative movement, opposed a synod that would define and delineate another new sect. The movement should grow naturally and spontaneously, he believed. However, in 1902, Schechter reorganized the now extremely influential seminary in New York, which had so struggled during its early years. One of Judaism's best-known and best-loved names within and outside Jewish circles, Abraham Joshua Heschel, taught at the seminary until his death.

Conservative synagogues today are a strong presence in American Jewry. With eighteen hundred synagogues nationwide, approximately two-fifths of American Jews affiliate with this branch of Judaism. Services are traditional, mostly in Hebrew and lasting two and one-half to three hours. As with each Judaic branch, they have their own individualized prayer book, with omissions and additions that are in line with Conservative beliefs. Many of the men, like the Orthodox, sway and bow spasmodically as they pray, which is said to increase concentration.

The Conservative movement trains women in their seminaries and ordains them as rabbis and cantors, though few women actually serve in these particular leadership positions. Some Conservative Jews may still hold to traditions that cause them to shy away from hiring a woman to lead their congregation, but primarily the lower number of female rabbis stems from the fact that fewer women in the Conservative movement are studying to become rabbis, compared to Reform; because the congregations are often smaller, fewer positions are available.

Still, women enjoy leadership privileges. They read Torah, which is a very honored position in Judaism. The Torah scroll read during a prayer service has been hand-written in Hebrew, with no vowels and no punctuation. It's very difficult to read. Lay-women who are called to read Torah sometimes send out informal announcements to their friends and families to let them know which Sabbath they will be reading. It's a very exciting time and one for which they've spent long hours of study and preparation.

Women are allowed to wear tallit and tefillin, though most don't; it's required for Conservative men. At Ahavath Sholom in Fort Worth, where my nephew attends Hebrew school, a sign at the entrance of the sanctuary reads, "Men are required to wear a tallit; women may also." Again, this *is* a step forward for women because women traditionally do not wear the tallit, tefillin, or even *kippot,* and it's a great honor to do so.

The Conservatives with whom I've studied have been extremely knowledgeable about all of their holy texts, and discussions in their study groups are lively and incredibly in-depth, raising twice as many questions as answers about a text, a very Jewish approach to study.

Although Conservatives see *halakhah* as mandatory, not optional, they also struggle—and succeed—to come up with liberal interpretations and applications. Many drive on Sabbath and have less strict definitions for keeping kosher than do the Orthodox. For many Jews, the Conservative movement is a happy medium—cherishing their ancient traditions while honoring the changes that new cultures and times demand.

Traditional

We troublesome women were, basically, the cause of a third movement in Judaism—Traditional—which broke off from the Conservative movement, which broke off from Reform. Traditional Jews severed ties with the Conservatives when the latter began admitting women to their seminary for rabbinical studies.

A service in a Traditional synagogue resembles the Orthodox, except that women and men may sit together if they choose. There are also separate sections marked "men only" and "women only," but they're usually in the same room. Otherwise, the services are about three hours long and, except for the sermon, are entirely in Hebrew. Women do not wear tallit or tefillin, and they do not read Torah or hold ordained leadership positions in synagogue.

Like all traditional Hebrew services, those three hours of prayer on Saturday morning are riveting in their intensity and deep spirituality. The men draped in their ornate prayer shawls dip, sway, and snap their bodies forward and back, wrapped in the tallit, rapt in God. Many of them stand here each and every morning at dawn, praying. They have recited these same prayers thousands of times and read precisely the same portion of Torah year after year, but watching them, it's impossible to doubt that they are praying and worshiping as if it were their very first encounter with God.

Tiferet Israel—the Traditional synagogue in Dallas—has become a center for many Jewish activities. Each year they host a kosher chili cook-off, and hundreds of people from all parts of the Jewish community participate. I attend every year and have worked a booth in the past. The vibrancy of this synagogue is obvious. At a recent, all-night Jewish holiday celebration, I popped in on them at 3 A.M. and the room was filled with animated study and conversation, with at least half of the participants eager, involved teenagers. In addition, Tiferet's rabbi provided a place of leadership for a female friend of mine, even though she was studying to become a rabbi under the auspices of a liberal branch of Judaism.

Traditional Judaism enjoys a strong place in the Jewish community. It provides everything that the Orthodox offer without the strict separation of men and women. It's a movement that embraces tradition while allowing Jewish women to feel closer to the heart of the service. Women in Traditional synagogues are physically close to the goings-on of the service. They touch Torah and aren't separated by a *mechitza*. And like all those who attend Jewish services, they are there to pray.

"Dayeanu," as Jews say during Pesach (Passover). It is enough for them. It is enough.

Orthodox

Not long ago, several people in my Sunday school class decided they were going to visit an Orthodox synagogue. This startled me. Even though Reform may be used to and comfortable with occasional Christian guests, the Orthodox certainly aren't. I e-mailed my friends and tried to prepare them: Did they know the women would be entering a different door from the men? Were they aware they shouldn't offer their hand to the rabbi to shake? What about prayers that shouldn't be interrupted, handbags not carried, cars parked across the street?

Yet perhaps I shouldn't have worried. Although there *are* things that are disrespectful to Orthodox Jews, they've always been gracious and forgiving of my own fax paus.

The Orthodox, of course, hold to the strictest level of ritual observance. They regard it, as do all Jews, as a means to draw closer to God, but the Orthodox believe that *halakhah* is obligatory. The men attend prayer services each day, walking to synagogue, many of them wearing black fedoras and black coats, though this isn't always the case. Married women often cover their heads, though again, this varies.

The Orthodox themselves have a fairly distinct split among themselves. On the one hand, there are "modern" Orthodox who believe in secular education as well as religious. They're more involved in American society as a whole and may not dress as conservatively, and some of the men may shake hands with women (think Joe Liebermann).

Other Orthodox are far more strict. At the Jewish holiday of Shavuot, for instance, when I was looking for different synagogues in which to study, I was turned away at one Orthodox synagogue. No women allowed. At another Orthodox service, however, I was told I'd be welcome to attend during any part of the evening.

Orthodox services are about three hours long and, except for the sermon, are entirely in Hebrew. Women usually enter a different door and sit in a different section of the room. Although it isn't forbidden for them to touch Torah, Torah isn't brought to the women's section, nor can they enter the men's, so they don't have this privilege.

Still, I love attending their services. At Shaare-Tefilla—one of the Orthodox synagogues I've attended—the atmosphere is worshipful, and I've learned to follow the order of the service a little better. Occasionally, when I'm certain it's appropriate, I've asked for minor interpretations of a phrase or ritual: Why, for instance, would a single woman stand up during certain parts of the service? It was explained to me that it's a Middle Eastern custom for a woman to stand when her husband or father reads Torah.

One little boy in a black coat and black fedora (this is unusual; men usually replace their hats with yarmulkes at the door of the sanctuary), who looked to be around eight or nine, sat in the back of the room, rising from time to time, swaying or bowing spasmodically as he read Torah. I asked someone about him. "He's just a pious little boy," they told me.

This was the same synagogue I attended when, during a young woman's bat mitzvah ceremony, the men shouted words of encouragement to her and the rabbi told her she would surely go to Harvard or Columbia, so deep and wide was her message.

Hasidim

Finally, there are the Hasidim. Although I've gone into enough detail throughout my book on this group that you should have a good idea what they're all about, here's a summary.

The Hasidim are referred to by many as the ultra-Orthodox, though I've avoided this term out of respect for them because they themselves don't like that term. Hasidim keep the highest level of observance regarding Jewish law, and some groups live in isolation from society. However, some Hasidim are, in some ways, often more tolerant and inclusive than some Orthodox.

The Hasidim are the mystical branch of Judaism, and their interpretations of Torah are based on kabbalah (the mystical texts of Judaism), as well as on Talmud. In addition, their services are exuberant, as one of the primary reasons the Hasidim formed was to bring new life and heart to Jewish ritual.

Although men and women are separated by a *mechitza* in Chabad, the Lubavitcher synagogue, it's usually a small, portable divider; the rabbi carries Torah down the women's aisle, allowing them to touch and kiss it. At breaks during the service, husbands and wives sometimes talk over the *mechitza,* and children run from one side of the room to the other.

Most of the people who attend Chabad aren't, in fact, Hasidic; they attend because they know little about Judaism and it's a friendly place for a Jew to learn how to become more observant.

This is Chabad, however. Although they're the outreach-to-Jews group of Hasidim, most other Hasidic groups are far more isolated. Most live in segregated communities, primarily in New York. By and large, they're uninterested in becoming involved in

American society and don't associate with non-Jews, or even with Jews outside their own sect.

Male Hasidim, like the Orthodox, wear long beards, black fedoras, and long black coats. Unlike the Orthodox, though, Hasidic males wear *peios,* or side curls. The women dress conservatively, with hems below the knee; depending on where they live, they might wear bright, modern colors.

The Hasidic rabbis I've studied with, from three different Hasidic sects, have been warm and accepting of me. Evidently, even in the world of Chassidus, some are more "modern" than others. I'm very grateful for that, for they've deeply enriched my life and heightened my love for and understanding of a faith perhaps unparalleled in its beauty and depth.

GLOSSARY

Aleinu   Prayer evoking a time of messianic harmony.

Amidah   The central anthology of prayers in a Jewish service. It is recited silently while standing.

Ark   The cabinet or chest where the Torah scrolls are kept.

Bar *or* **bat mitzvah**   Literally, "son" or "daughter of the commandment," a ceremony marking the time when children become responsible for fulfilling Jewish commandments and take their place in the adult community.

Chabad   The community of Lubavitchers, including their synagogue and various activities.

Challah   A braided egg bread traditionally used on the Sabbath and other occasions.

Chevruta   (Aramaic) A study partner.

Gabbai   A rabbinical assistant or synagogue treasurer.

Gemara   Commentary on the Mishnah; part of the Talmud.

Halakhah   Jewish law.

Hasidism   A mystical sect of Orthodox Judaism that places emphasis on bringing passion and heart to Jewish ritual.

Havurah   A small study or worship group.

Kabbalah   The Jewish mystical tradition.

Kavanah   Intent. When a prayer is recited or a ritual done with *kavanah*, it's done with the heart.

Kiddush   The blessing recited over the wine each Sabbath and on other holy days.

Kippah   Hebrew for "skullcap" (plural is *kippot*); in Yiddish it is called a *yarmulke*.

Kohen   Priest.

Kosher   Literally: ritually fit or acceptable.

Lubavitch   A Hasidic sect of Judaism that "outreaches" to other Jews, helping them become more observant of Jewish law.

Mechitza   The divider between men and women used in Orthodox synagogues.

Menorah   Technically a Hanukiah, a nine-branched candelabrum used during Hanukkah. A seven-branched variety often adorns synagogues.

Menuha   Hebrew for rest.

Midrash   Writings, including stories, commentaries, parables, and other interpretive materials which expand the Biblical text.

Mikvah   The ritual bath used by Orthodox women after their menstrual cycle and as a part of conversion to Judaism.

Mitzvah   Although sometimes used as a euphemism for "good deed," it actually means "command." Plural is *mitzvot*.

Parsha   The Torah portion (or lection) of the week. The Torah is divided into 54 parshiyot.

Rebbe   A Hasidic leader or spiritual guide who is almost always also a rabbi.

Sefer Torah   A Torah scroll that has been hand-written on a parchment scroll.

Shekhinah   The divine, feminine in-dwelling presence of God.

Shema   Deuteronomy 6:4: "Hear, O Israel: the Lord is our God, the Lord is the One and Only."

Shochet   A ritual butcher, whose techniques ensure that the animal's life is taken in holiness.

Shul   Synagogue.

Tallit   The prayer shawl worn during morning prayer services.

Talmud A book consisting of Mishnah, or Oral Law, and the Gemara, a commentary on the Mishnah.

Tanakh The Hebrew Bible. *Tanakh* is an acronym for *Torah* (law), *Neviim* (prophets), and *Ketubim* (writings).

Tefillin Two small black leather boxes worn one on the head and the other on the left hand, during morning prayer services except on the Sabbath and holidays. The boxes contain scripture and are considered to be required by four passages in the Torah that command that the scripture be a "sign upon thy hand and a frontlet between thine eyes."

Tzaddik A Jewish holy person; a saint.

Yeshiva A Jewish seminary.

YHVH The most holy name of God. Many Jews, particularly the Orthodox, neither pronounce this name nor add vowels to it. It's known as the tetragrammaton.

RECOMMENDED READING

Buxbaum, Yitzhak. *Jewish Tales of Mystic Joy.* San Francisco: Jossey-Bass, 2002.

Cahill, Thomas. *The Gifts of the Jews.* New York: Anchor Books, 1998.

Cunningham, Philip A., and Starr, Arthur F. (eds.). *Sharing Shalom.* Mahwah, N.J.: Paulist Press, 1998.

Freeman, Tzvi. *Bringing Heaven down to Earth.* Holbrook, Mass.: Adams Media, 1999.

Heschel, Abraham Joshua. *The Sabbath.* New York: Farrar, Straus & Giroux, 1951.

Heschel, Abraham Joshua. *God in Search of Man.* Northvale, N.J.: Aronson, 1987.

Kushner, Lawrence. *Eyes Remade for Wonder.* Woodstock, Vt.: Jewish Lights, 1998.

Olitzky, Kerry M., and Judson, Daniel. *The Rituals and Practices of a Jewish Life.* Woodstock, Vt.: Jewish Lights, 2002.

Pressman, Kati. *Shabbos Candles.* Boulder, Colo.: Jester Press, 1995.

Scholem, Gershom. *Origins of the Kabbalah.* New York: Jewish Publication Society, 1987.

Vermes, Geza. *Jesus and the World of Judaism.* Minneapolis: Augsburg Fortress, 1983.

Vermes, Geza. *The Religion of Jesus the Jew.* Minneapolis: Augsburg Fortress, 1993.

Wiesel, Elie. *Sages and Dreamers.* New York: Summit Books, 1991.

NOTES

Chapter One

1.   Kushner, 1998, p. 49.

2.   Out of respect for the Jews, I've begun to refer to the two testaments as "Hebrew" and "Greek," respectively, identifying them by the language in which they were likely first written.

3.   The Hasidim, as well as the more conservative Orthodox, don't shake hands with women who aren't close relatives due to certain rules they follow regarding sexual purity.

Chapter Two

1.   Myerhoff, 1978, p. 126.

2.   Wiesel, 1991, pp. 364–366.

3.   Kushner, 1998, p. 59.

4.   Gordis, 1995, pp. 157, 158.

5.   The prohibition against cooking a "kid in the milk of its mother" is repeated three times in the Torah: Exodus 23:19 and 34:26 and Deuteronomy 14:21. Later rabbinical decrees expanded this into a Jewish law that forbade mixing meat and dairy products.

6.   Driver, 1991, p. 97.

7.   Heschel, 1966, pp. 8, 10, 22.

Chapter Three

1.   Adilman, 2000b.

2.   Hammer, 1999, p. 106.

3.   Pollak, 1980, p. 69ff.

Chapter Four

1. Heschel, 1987, p. xxxiii.
2. Buber, 1966, p. 53.
3. Wiesel, 1993, p. 108.
4. Kamin, 1990, p. 225.
5. Adilman, 2000a.
6. Kittel, 1964, p. 180.
7. *Encyclopedia Judaica,* 1997.
8. N. E. Goldstein, 2000, p. 48.
9. Many Orthodox don't write vowels in any name of God because they see it as disrespectful to discard anything with a name of God or any writing of Torah. Some exclude the English word *God,* but others don't. Inserting a hyphen avoids writing, and thus discarding, a name of God. Because this was a direct quote from an Orthodox Jew, I wrote "G-d" as he wrote it.
10. Steinberg, 1947, p. 41.
11. Howe, 1999, pp. 9–10.
12. Heschel, 1987, p. 64.
13. *The Book of Concealed Mystery,* 2000, pp. 22, 23, 29.
14. Kushner, 1998, p. 142.
15. Moshiach, 2000.
16. Lew and Jaffe, 1999, p. 215.

Chapter Five

1. "Three Weeks," 2000.
2. E. Goldstein, 2000.
3. Balin, 1997, p. 1.
4. Balin, 1997, p. 10.
5. Gillman, 2000, p. 12.
6. Monroe, 1998, p. xiii.

Chapter Six

1. Eisenberg, 1995, p. 2.
2. Birnbaum, 2000.
3. Wiesel, 1993, p. 103.
4. Wiesel, 1993, p. 221.
5. Wiesel, 1968, p. 151.
6. Gershom, 2001, p. 5.
7. Wiesel, 1993, p. 50.
8. Meizlish, 1997, pp. 47–56.
9. Eliach, 1982, pp. 3, 4.
10. Eliach, 1982, pp. 3, 4.
11. Weissman, 1985, p. 8.

12. Godwin, 2001, p. 268.

13. For the most part, Sufism is the mystical branch of Islam, though there are some "universal" orders that seek to incorporate the principles of Sufism without affiliating with any particular religion.

14. Gershom, 2001, p. 4.

15. Fishkoff, 2000, pp. 45–53.

16. There are two accepted spellings, *Bratslav* and *Breslov,* the former being perhaps more common; the latter is the spelling used by the Breslovers themselves.

17. Green, 1981, pp. 4, 7, 10, 14.

18. Eisenberg, 1995, p. 171.

19. Lew and Jaffe, 1999, p. 265.

20. Tanya, July 12, 2000.

21. Tanya, July 24, 2000.

22. Lew and Jaffe, 1999, p. 282.

23. *The Book of Concealed Mystery,* 2000, p. 21.

24. Kazantzakis, 1952, p. 296.

Chapter Seven

1. The doctrine of supercession regards Judaism as having been replaced by Christianity, the Jews having been rejected by God in favor of those who accept Jesus as their Messiah. The Catholic church, as well as many evangelical churches, have begun to reject this doctrine.

2. Eck, 1993, p. 42.

3. Ner-David, 2000, p. 15.

4. Broshi, 1999.

5. Vermes, 1993, p. 24.

6. Vermes, 1993, p. 21.

7. Neusner, 1994, p. 63.

8. Harrelson and Falk, 1990, pp. 9, 10.

9. Packer, 2000.

10. Milgram, 2000.

11. Soc.Culture.Jewish, 2003.

12. Harrelson and Falk, 1990, pp. 20, 21.

13. "The Church's Agony," May 3, 2002.

14. Lapin, 2002.

15. *Nightline,* 1999.

Chapter Eight

1. Muller, 1999, p. 186.

2. Freeman, 2002.

3. Cahill, 1998, p. 3.

4.   Boman, 1960, pp. 17, 27.
5.   Pressman, 1995, n.p.
6.   Remen, 2000, p. 6.
7.   Gold, 1987.

Judaism 101

1.   In trying to come up with a word that satisfies everyone, I've fallen short. Some say I shouldn't divide Jews or Judaism. Some say "Traditional" is a movement; others say it isn't. The Union for Traditional Judaism states that it's a "trans-denominational education and outreach organization dedicated to promoting the principles of traditional Judaism." When I phoned the organization, they simply said that I probably won't find a word that makes everyone happy. The fact that they have synagogues called Traditional and differ in distinctive ways from other branches of Judaism, however, makes me comfortable in calling it a movement.

2.   ALEPH, n.d.
3.   Friedman, 1999, p. 10.

REFERENCES

Adilman, B. *B'ohalei Tzaddikim—Parshas Shemini/HaChodesh* 5760. Available on-line at www.barak-online.net. Mar. 28, 2000a.

Adilman, B. *B'Ohalei Tzaddikim—Parshas Bechukosai* 5760. Available on-line at www.barak-online.net. May 26, 2000b.

ALEPH: Alliance for Jewish Renewal. "Frequently Asked Questions About Jewish Renewal." n.d. Available on-line at www.aleph.org/html/faq.html.

Balin, C. B. "From Periphery to Center: A History of the Women's Rabbinic Network." *CCAR Journal,* Summer 1997, pp. 1–12.

Birnbaum, B. "How to Pray: Reverence, Stories and the Rebbe's Dream." *Image: A Journal of the Arts,* 2000, *27,* 66–78.

Boman, T. *Hebrew Thought Compared with Greek.* New York: Norton, 1960.

The Book of Concealed Mystery (part of *Zohar*). "Ways of Mysticism" Series. New York: Delian Bower, 2000.

Broshi, M. "The Jewish Jesus." *Jerusalem Post Internet Edition,* Feb. 2, 1999. Available on-line at www.jpost.com.

Buber, M. *Way of Response.* New York: Schocken Books, 1966.

Cahill, T. *Gifts of the Jews.* New York: Anchor Books, 1998.

"The Church's Agony." *Forward* (editorial), May 3, 2002.

Driver, T. F. *The Magic of Ritual.* San Francisco: HarperSanFrancisco, 1991.

Eck, D. L. *Encountering God.* Boston: Beacon Press, 1993.

Eisenberg, R. *Boychiks in the Hood.* San Francisco: HarperSanFrancisco, 1995.

Eliach, Y. *Hasidic Tales of the Holocaust.* New York: Oxford University Press, 1982.

Encyclopedia Judaica (CD-ROM). Jerusalem: Judaica Multimedia (Israel) Ltd., 1997.

Fishkoff, S. "Black Hat Blitz." *Moment,* Aug. 2000.

Freeman, T. "Daily Dose." Apr. 24, 2002. Available on-line at www.chabad.org.

Friedman, R. S. "The Emergence of Reconstructionism: An Evolving American Judaism, 1922–1945." American Jewish Archives, 1999. Available on-line at huc.edu/aja/Fried.html.

Gershom, Y. "FAQ on Hasidism (Chassidism)—PART 1-A OF 3." Available on-line at pinenet.com/~rooster/hasid1.html. Mar. 26, 2001.

Gillman, N. *Encountering God in Judaism.* "The Way Into" Series. Woodstock, Vt.: Jewish Lights, 2000.

Godwin, G. *Heart.* New York: Morrow, 2001.

Gold, S. *Birkat HaMazon.* 1987. Available on-line at rabbishefagold.com.

Goldstein, E. (ed.). *The Women's Torah Commentary.* Woodstock, Vt.: Jewish Lights, 2000.

Goldstein, N. E. *God at the Edge.* New York: Bell Tower, 2000.

Gordis, D. *God Was Not in the Fire.* New York: Scribner, 1995.

Green, A. *Tormented Master: A Life of Rabbi Nahman of Bratslav.* New York: Schocken Books, 1981.

Hammer, J. *Chosen by God.* New York: Hyperion, 1999.

Harrelson, W., and Falk, R. M. *Jews and Christians: A Troubled Family.* Nashville, Tenn.: Abingdon Press, 1990.

Heschel, A. J. *Man's Quest for God.* New York: Scribner, 1954.

Heschel, A. J. *The Sabbath.* New York: HarperCollins, 1966.

Heschel, A. J. *God in Search of Man.* Mahwah, N.J.: Aronson, 1987.

Howe, M. B. "Judaism: Finding Our Roots." *Mars Hill Review,* Summer 1999, pp. 9–10.

Kamin, B. *Stones in the Soul.* Old Tappan, N.J.: Macmillan, 1990.

Kazantzakis, N. *Zorba the Greek.* New York: Touchstone, 1952.

Kittel, G. (ed.). *Theological Dictionary of the New Testament.* Grand Rapids, Mich.: Eerdmans, 1964.

Kushner, L. *Eyes Remade for Wonder.* Woodstock, Vt.: Jewish Lights, 1998.

Lapin, D. "Born-Again Allies." *Forward,* June 21, 2002.

Lew, A., and Jaffe, S. *One God Clapping.* Woodstock, Vt.: Jewish Lights, 1999.

Meizlish, A. *Chasidic Stories Made in Heaven.* Brooklyn, N.Y.: Otsar Sifrei Lubavitch, 1997.

Milgram, G. "Seminary and Homosexuality Policies." Available on-line at shamash.org. Mar. 29, 2000.

Monroe, D. *The Lost Books of Merlyn.* St. Paul, Minn.: Llewellyn, 1998.

"Moshiach in the Weekly Torah Portion." Available on-line at chabad.org. Oct. 17, 2000.

Muller, W. *Sabbath.* New York: Bantam Books, 1999.

Myerhoff, B. *Number Our Days.* New York: Simon & Schuster, 1978.

Nightline. "Aunt Rosie's Kitchen." Television broadcast. ABC News, Dec. 15, 1999.

Ner-David, H. *Life on the Fringes.* Needham, Mass.: JFL Books, 2000.

Packer, J. "Jews Turning to Online Matchmakers." *Dallas Morning News,* May 27, 2000, p. 1G.

Pollak, M. *Mandarins, Jews, and Missionaries.* New York: Weatherhill, 1980.

Pressman, K. *Shabbos Candles.* Boulder, Colo.: Jester Press, 1995.

Remen, R. N. *My Grandfather's Blessings.* New York: Riverhead Books, 2000.

Soc.Culture.Jewish Newsgroups. "FAQ: Question 18.3.9: Reform's Position on . . . Intermarriage." Available on-line at http://shamash.org/lists/scj-faq/html. Feb. 1, 2003.

Steinberg, M. *Basic Judaism.* Orlando, Fla.: Harcourt Brace, 1947.

"Tanya for Wednesday, 9 Tamuz 5760—July 12, 2000." Available on-line at chabad.org.

"Tanya for Monday, 21 Tamuz 5706—July 24, 2000." Available on-line at chabad.org.

"The Three Weeks: Rachel: The Story of Redemption." July 31, 2000. Available on-line at www.aish.com/holidays/tisha_bav_and_the_3_weeks/last/rachel.asp

Vermes, G. *The Religion of Jesus the Jew.* Minneapolis: Augsburg Fortress, 1993.

Weissman, M. *The Midrash Says: The Book of Devarim.* New York: Bnay Yakov, 1985.

Wiesel, E. *Legends of Our Time.* New York: Schocken Books, 1968.

Wiesel, E. *Sages and Dreamers.* New York: Summit Books, 1991.

Wiesel, E. *Souls on Fire.* New York: Touchstone, 1993.

THE AUTHOR

Mary Blye Howe's writing has been published in numerous periodicals, including the *Chicago Tribune, Mars Hill Review, Guideposts,* and the *Dallas Morning News.* Her speaking engagements have included churches, writing conferences, and schools. She was formerly the Dallas–Fort Worth president of Christians for Biblical Equality. Though she loves to hike, play classical guitar, and travel, her greatest love is finding new "spiritual adventures"—experiencing God through the eyes of people from other religions and cultures. She graduated summa cum laude from the University of Texas at Arlington and holds a degree in philosophy and anthropology.

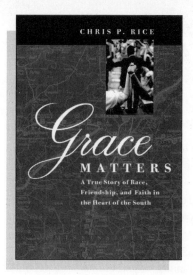

Grace Matters:
A True Story of Race, Friendship, and Faith in the Heart of the South

Chris P. Rice

$22.95 Hardcover
ISBN: 0–7879–5704–6

"Grace is the most potent counterforce at work in our violent species, and our only hope. Chris Rice gives a very personal account, at once inspiring and disturbing, of its transforming power."

—PHILIP YANCEY, author, *What's So Amazing About Grace?*, *Soul Survivor,* and *Where Is God When It Hurts?*

AMERICANS FEEL fatigued by racial divisions yet yearn to resolve them, to somehow live together in greater harmony and understanding. We all want a powerful story of success and hope, showing us that true racial reconciliation is indeed possible. This book tells that story. Imbued with the passion of his Christian faith, white college student Chris Rice left his studies at Middlebury College in Vermont to join the Voice of Calvary ministry in a tough urban neighborhood in Jackson, Mississippi. There he met Spencer Perkins, eldest son of John Perkins, legendary African American evangelist and civil rights movement activist.

In *Grace Matters,* Chris tells the story of this remarkable interracial faith community where he and Spencer and a dedicated group of black and white Christians worked together to realize the vision of the Sermon on the Mount and in so doing improve the impoverished lives of people in their neighborhood. At Antioch, as they called the community they founded, several families pooled all their resources and lives and set out on a journey to racial reconciliation and fidelity to their faith and its power.

For all those who wonder whether true racial reconciliation is possible, in this moving, powerful book Chris Rice shows that it is—but only with the help of God's grace and the dedication of those who seek the personal breakthroughs that can only be achieved by not giving up on each other, no matter what.

CHRIS P. RICE is currently pursuing studies at the Divinity School at Duke University. He is the winner of a Critic's Choice Award from *Christianity Today* magazine for his book *More Than Equals: Racial Healing for the Sake of the Gospel,* which he coauthored with Spencer Perkins. He has been a research associate for the Boston University Institute on Race and Social Division, a columnist for *Sojourners* magazine, and has written, spoken, and taught extensively on the subject of racial reconciliation.

[Price subject to change]

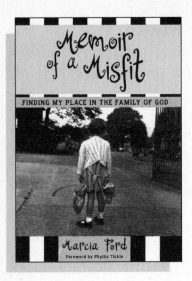

Memoir of a Misfit:
Finding My Place in the Family of God
Marcia Ford

$18.95 Hardcover
ISBN: 0–7879–6399–2

How many of us have, in Marcia Ford's words, "sacrificed pieces of (ourselves)" to find acceptance in the church? How many of us have suppressed our true stories, gifts, and even intelligence for the sake of fitting in? Marcia Ford's *Memoir of a Misfit* is the candid, delightfully irreverent journey of a woman determined not to settle for recycled faith.
—Sally Morgenthaler, author, *Worship Evangelism* and founder, Sacramentis.com

MARCIA FORD's funny, fresh, and frank memoir chronicles the spiritual journey of a self-proclaimed misfit. Like Anne Lamott, she is witty, quirky, and candid about her shortcomings and her sneaking suspicion that she may really be a square peg in a round hole. Equally reminiscent of Lamott's writing, it is through Ford's own uniqueness (her so-called misfittedness) that she is able to discover and claim God's abundant grace, and come to experience God more fully.

Like the author, many of us, especially women, feel as if we don't quite "belong"— not in society, due to seismic cultural shifts, and not even in the church. *Memoir of a Misfit* will help fellow misfits everywhere appreciate (and even relish) God's purpose in making us the way He did. Specific scriptures, when viewed from the perspective of a misfit, coupled with personal experience and the wisdom of others, underscore the value of misfits and the special place we all have in the family of God.

MARCIA FORD is a writer, principal in WordSpring Media, and contributor to *Publisher Weekly's* Religion BookLine. She has been an editor for *Charisma, Christian Retailing, Ministries Today,* and iBelieve.com. She resides near Orlando, Florida, with her husband and children.

[Price subject to change]